FORM 19

DEMCO

MAR - - 2002

SATANISM

Other books in the At Issue series:

SATANISM

Tamara L. Roleff, *Book Editor*

Daniel Leone, *President*
Bonnie Szumski, *Publisher*
Scott Barbour, *Managing Editor*
Stuart B. Miller, *Series Editor*

An Opposing Viewpoints® Series

Greenhaven Press, Inc.
San Diego, California

Library of Congress Cataloging-in-Publication Data

Satanism / Tamara L. Roleff, book editor.
    p. cm. — (At issue)
    Includes bibliographical references and index.
    ISBN 0-7377-0806-9 (pbk. : alk. paper) —
ISBN 0-7377-0807-7 (lib. bdg. : alk. paper)
    1. Satanism. I. Roleff, Tamara L., 1959– II. At issue (San Diego, Calif.)

BF1548 .S37   2002
133.4'22—dc21   2001040612
                                                          CIP

© 2002 by Greenhaven Press, Inc.
10911 Technology Place, San Diego, CA 92127

Printed in the U.S.A.

Every effort has been made to trace owners of copyrighted material.

Table of Contents

Page

Introduction

Satan and his various manifestations have been worshiped and revered for thousands of years. However, many people are confused over what makes one a Satanist. Some people think that anyone who believes in any religion other than their own is worshipping Satan, while others believe that any religion other than Christianity, Judaism, or Islam is Satanism. Still others believe that such religions as Santeria, Wicca, New Age, Druidism, and other neopagan religions are Satanism. However, true Satanists are none of the above.

Contemporary Satanism began April 30, 1966 when Anton Szandor LaVey, a former carnival barker, founded the Church of Satan in San Francisco. LaVey wrote books titled *The Satanic Bible, The Compleat Witch* (later revised as *The Satanic Witch*), and *The Satanic Rituals* to explain his view of Satanism. According to LaVey, Satanists have an entirely different vision of Satan than Christians do: Satan does not live in or rule Hell; he does not have horns, cloven hooves, a tail, and a pitchfork; and he is not evil. Nor do Satanists worship him as a living deity; the Church of Satan explains that "Satan is used as a purely symbolic figure. . . . Satanists do not even believe in the existence of any Gods or Devils." Instead, the church maintains that Satan is a force of energy, power, and sexuality, and a symbol of vitality, pleasure, and hedonism. Satanism is "essentially a religion of the self; it holds that the individual and his personal needs comes first," LaVey asserts. In fact, the holiest day for a Satanist is his or her own birthday.

The core beliefs of Satanism are found in the Nine Satanic Statements, written by LaVey in *The Satanic Bible*. They are:
1. Satan represents indulgence instead of abstinence!
2. Satan represents vital existence instead of spiritual pipe dreams!
3. Satan represents undefiled wisdom instead of hypocritical self-deceit!
4. Satan represents kindness to those who deserve it instead of love wasted on ingrates!
5. Satan represents vengeance instead of turning the other cheek!
6. Satan represents responsibility to the responsible instead of concern for psychic vampires!
7. Satan represents man as just another animal, sometimes better, more often worse than those that walk on all-fours, who, because of his "divine spiritual and intellectual development," has become the most vicious animal of all!
8. Satan represents all of the so-called sins, as they all lead to physical, mental, or emotional gratification!
9. Satan has been the best friend the Church has ever had, as He has kept it in business all these years!

However, not all Satanists necessarily believe or follow all of these statements; since Satanism worships the self, it is a highly individualistic religion and the beliefs may vary widely from one Satanist to the next. Satanism is recognized as a religion in the United States; the U.S. Army, for example, includes Satanism in its pamphlet, *Religious Requirements and Practices of Certain Selected Groups: A Handbook for Chaplains.* Although it is difficult to determine how many people are Satanists (the Church of Satan does not release membership information), the Army handbook estimated that there were between 10,000 and 20,000 Satanists in the United States when it was published in 1978.

Most Satanists are adults who are serious about their beliefs. But Satanism also attracts teenagers, who are frequently "dabblers"—that is, as an act of rebellion against their parents or society, they practice Satanism, usually for a short period of time. These teen Satanists' numbers are almost impossible to count as they do not belong to any organized satanic church (most organized satanic churches—such as the Church of Satan—require that members be eighteen years old to join). These dabblers sometimes engage in criminal activity such as vandalism and grave desecration, trespassing, and consumption of alcohol and illegal drugs. Researchers who study teen Satanists contend that the thrill of law-breaking makes Satanism even more exciting to them.

Many people, especially conservative Christians, view Satanism and Satanists as far more threatening, however. Their concerns are based on Gothic Satanism, which first appeared during the Middle Ages. According to Church leaders of the time, Satanists were evil incarnate: They sold their souls to the devil, killed children in ritual ceremonies, changed shapes between animals and humans, flew on broomsticks, conducted Black Masses, and performed black magic to harm others. Some people believe that Satanists continue to practice many of these evil deeds, especially human sacrifice and ritual abuse.

The first modern accounts of satanic ritual abuse and satanic human sacrifice appeared during the late 1970s and continued into the early 1990s. Since then, the reports have tapered off. The first cases consisted of several women who came forward independently and reported that they had recovered long-repressed memories of their sexual abuse and torture as children by satanic groups, some of which included members of their families. These women were from different parts of the country, yet their stories of sexual abuse, ritual murder of babies, cannibalism, and blood drinking were very similar. Then children in day care centers across the country began telling comparable stories of how they were sexually abused, were witnesses to murders in hidden rooms, and were forced to eat feces and the flesh of victims.

In response to these claims, some therapists, law enforcement, and judicial officials theorized that an extremely organized secret network of Satanists was responsible for the violence. They estimated that Satanists were performing—and getting away with—as many as 50,000 ritual murders every year. Furthermore, they claimed, leaders of the conspiracy were noted members of the community—government and law enforcement officials, teachers, lawyers, and doctors. Because of their importance in the community, these leaders were able to keep their satanic activities secret.

Occasionally, child molesters, serial killers, and other criminals claim to be Satanists, asserting that "the Devil made me do it" or that they killed for the glory of Satan. Some infamous killers who claim to be Satanists include Charles Manson, "Son of Sam" serial killer David Berkowitz, and "Night Stalker" Richard Ramirez. Ramirez carved a pentagram—a star with five points that is a symbol of Satanism—into his left hand and left court one day shouting "Hail Satan!"

Satanists claim, however, that Gothic Satanism is a myth that was spread by church officials in the Middle Ages to frighten and persecute personal enemies and anyone who was different. Modern Satanists assert, in fact, that their religion expressly forbids human or animal sacrifice. According to LaVey, "Satanism respects and exalts life. Children and animals are the purest expressions of that life force, and as such are held sacred and precious." Therefore, he adds, it would be very unsatanic to sacrifice or abuse either children or animals.

Many law enforcement officials have carefully investigated claims of satanic abuse and ritual murder and have not found any evidence that these crimes—as described by the survivors—have been committed. Kenneth V. Lanning, a supervisory special agent with the FBI's Behavioral Science Unit in Quantico, Virginia, studied reports of satanic ritual abuse and ritual murder and concluded in a 1992 report that it is extremely unlikely that the claims of ritual abuse and murder are true: "If and when members of a destructive cult commit murders, they are bound to make mistakes, leave evidence, and eventually make admissions in order to brag about their crimes or reduce their legal liability." He adds that law enforcement officials searched for evidence for eight years and found "little or no evidence" to support claims of satanic ritual abuse and ritual murder. He adds:

> Until hard evidence is obtained and corroborated, the public should not be frightened into believing that babies are being bred and eaten, that 50,000 missing children are being murdered in human sacrifices, or that satanists are taking over America's day care centers or institutions.

Satanism is a frightening religion to many people, and sometimes out of their fear come bizarre claims and allegations. *At Issue: Satanism* examines some of these claims and provides a broad perspective of what Satanism is and the controversies surrounding its beliefs and practices.

1

Satanism Threatens Youth

Elizabeth Karlsberg

Elizabeth Karlsberg is a freelance writer.

Law enforcement officials across the country have discovered connections between teenage Satanists and many crimes. Satanism threatens America and its youth because it reverses good and bad so that evil is worshiped and goodness is reviled. Some teens are attracted to Satanism because they falsely believe that it gives them control over their lives. Many Satanists abuse drugs and alcohol; they also suffer from low self-esteem and a sense of not belonging. Telltale signs of youthful involvement in Satanism are given.

While there are no hard statistics to indicate just how many teens have fallen prey to Satan's evil messages, law enforcement authorities all over the country have uncovered the telltale signs of Satanism in connection to many crime cases:

• An inverted pentagram or upside-down five-pointed star. (A pentagram right-side up is a symbol of "white magic.")
• The number 666, or the letters FFF, which stands for the sign of the Beast.
• A goat's head is the actual symbol for Satan.
• An upside-down cross, which signifies the rejection of Christianity, or, if you will, Christianity turned on its head.

But it's not simply the appearance of Satanic symbols that have authorities concerned. It's the violent and bizarre incidents that have occurred across the nation—incidents that have indicated Satanists at work. Some nightmarish, but true, tales include:

• A 14-year-old student at York High School in Dupage County, Ill., who stabbed three students after being teased about his Satanic beliefs. Two of the victims were hospitalized. The boy reportedly carved an upside-down cross on his arm after being arrested.
• Two girls, ages 12 and 13, who carried out a Satanic murder-suicide pact in Montgomery County, Md. Both girls had told school friends they wanted to die so they could "meet Satan." Aspirin was the only drug detected in either girl's body.

Reprinted, with permission, from "Satanism: The Scary Truth," by Elizabeth Karlsberg, *Teen*, June 1993.

• A 19-year-old young man who had practiced Satanism for at least four years was charged with killing his 38-year-old mother. Police and medical reports show that she had been stabbed 40 times. Her throat had also been slit.

These gruesome accounts are just a few that have been recorded by The Cult Awareness Network (CAN), based in Chicago. This group is the only national, non-profit organization in the United States dedicated to helping those victimized by cults.

What is Satanism?

If you can imagine a world where good is bad and bad is good, then you've got some idea of what Satanists believe. At its root, Satanism is the perversion of religion.

With devil worship, there are no laws, no rules, no cannots. The founder of the Church of Satan, Anton LaVey, once said that "Instead of commanding members to repress their natural urges, we teach that they should follow them. This includes physical lust, the desire for revenge, the drive for material possessions."

At its root, Satanism is the perversion of religion.

Essentially, Satanism promises a lot for very little. It promises power over others and the forces that hold people back from having what they want. Its philosophy is as simple as this: Worship the devil; do his dirty work, and in return, he'll give you what you want.

And that's why some kids find Satanism so appealing. According to CAN executive director, Cynthia Kisser, "Satanism appears to offer easy answers to complex problems." By performing rituals, Satanists believe that they can control their lives, which may seem pretty out of control.

Who's turning to Satan?

Teens who get involved in Satanism often feel cut off from positive social outlets. Their sense of isolation may stem from alcoholism in the home. There may be some sort of physical, emotional abuse or neglect in the family. Or it could be simply that the parents haven't been able to communicate their values to their children.

"These kids have kind of been left adrift," explains Dr. Paul King, a child and adolescent psychiatrist and clinical assistant professor at the University of Tennessee, Memphis. "They're not in Scouts; they're not in any church youth group or any of these positive pro-social activities." Satanism then becomes a substitute for the positive influences that are missing in a teen's life.

The influence of drugs and low self-esteem

Experts agree: Drug and alcohol abuse seem to go hand-in-hand with Satanism. Kisser believes Satanism actually "serves as a justification of drug and alcohol abuse." David Toma says he's "never met a Satan worshiper who didn't do drugs."

Drug use complicates matters for teens who turn to devil worship, making it harder and harder to distinguish what's actually real and what only appears to be real when viewed through the fog of drugs and alcohol.

People—teens included—who feel the need to use drugs often do so because something in their lives is lacking. Often, that something is a good feeling about oneself.

Teens who have a good sense of self realize that they have control, or power, over their own lives. They don't need Satanism. Even if their friends are getting involved with it, they are able to say, "That's not for me." The sad truth is that those who don't feel good about themselves may look elsewhere for a sense of power. And since positive influences may be nonexistent—or unattainable—the negative ones look all the more inviting.

David's story

Sometimes, teens are simply searching for a place to belong, and Satanism provides an instant social circle to plug into. One such teen, David (not his real name) explains how he got involved in devil worship.

"I was never very popular . . . kind of kept to myself most of the time," says David. "One day at lunch, this guy came up to me. He seemed pretty cool, like he had it all together. He invited me to a party, and I decided to go.

"They were playing this weird music, and people were drinking and doing drugs," David recalls. "They all seemed to be having a good time. It wasn't until this guy took me into a room—painted black, with candles everywhere and these posters of skulls with wings and stuff, that I realized these people were into something different. Even though it kind of freaked me out, I felt like, hey, these people want me to be a part of them. It felt really good.

"Pretty soon, I was going to cemeteries with them, doing rituals. We'd dig up graves, cut up animals and hang them from trees. Some of the people would drink blood. I never got into that, but my grades started dropping, and I got into drugs.

"Eventually, my parents went ballistic. They said I couldn't hang out with these people anymore. Then they forced me to see a therapist. I'd go, but at first I'd just tell a bunch of lies. Then, I don't know how, but the therapist made me see how messed up I was and how my life wasn't better because of Satanism; my life was just a big lie."

Out of the darkness

While some experts feel that Satanism is on the decline, the problem is that it's just one destructive alternative. David Trahan, director of the Center for Ritualistic Deviance at Hart Grove Hospital in Chicago believes that, no matter what alternative teens are getting involved with, the first step is to help them see that "what they're involved with is not going to have the pay-off they're looking for."

Of course, the ultimate goal is to treat the reasons these kids were looking for some destructive alternative in the first place. In other words, you have to treat the cause, not the symptom, which may be Satanism.

Trahan feels that for teens to achieve this, they need to have the confidence instilled in them that they have a good shot at success using traditional means.

Before confronting someone you suspect is experimenting with Satanism, it's a good idea to get more information to see just how involved the person is. Don't take or move any of the items you might discover. For guidance, you can write to: Cult Awareness Network [1680 N. Vine, Suite 415, Los Angeles, CA 90028].

Recently, a rather troubling letter turned up in 'TEEN's mailbags. The person who sent the letter said that some people she was hanging around with were "getting into some weird stuff that involved Satan." The letter went on to describe some of that weird stuff, which included "rituals with animals," among some other pretty awful acts. Whoever sent the letter seemed genuinely concerned and wrote, "I don't want to hang around with these people anymore. What should I do?" The letter was signed, simply, "Frightened."

This letter, coupled with other things we'd read and heard about, left us wondering just how many teens are involved with Satanism. It didn't take much investigating to get an answer. The sad truth is, Satanism is a threat in this country.

David Toma, a former vice detective turned motivational speaker, has written about this threat in his latest book, *Turning Your Life Around: David Toma's Guide for Teenagers*. Toma says that in every school he speaks at, he asks the same question: "How many of you kids know someone or have heard of someone involved in Satanic practices?" He estimates that a full one-third of the students raise their hands. What's even more disturbing is that some of these teens get so caught up in worshiping the devil that they destroy their own lives.

This article is intended to increase teens' awareness of the dangers of Satanic cults. 'TEEN Magazine does not condone devil worship in any form, and we urge you to report any incidents you may be aware of to a trusted adult or the appropriate authorities.

Warning signs

If you suspect that someone you know is experimenting with Satanism, The Cult Awareness Network suggests that you look for a combination of behavior changes, such as:

- bitter hatred toward family and family religion
- drastic drop in grades from A's and B's to D's and F's
- cut marks on the body
- little or middle fingernail on left hand painted black (left is evil, right is good)
- involvement with alcohol or illegal drugs
- use of a Satanic nickname
- use of various alphabets such as Egyptian, witches or one of their own creation.

2

Satanists Worship Evil and Power

James Randall Noblitt and Pamela Sue Perskin

James Randall Noblitt is a clinical psychologist in Dallas, Texas, and director of the Center for Counseling and Psychological Services. Pamela Sue Perskin is the executive director of the International Council on Cultism and Ritual Trauma. They are the authors of Cult and Ritual Abuse: Its History, Anthropology, and Recent Discovery in Contemporary America.

Satanism is just one religion among many in which a deity is worshiped not because of goodness, but because of power. Many people worship Satan because the satanic rituals of abuse and torture give them a sense of power over their victims. The Satanist enjoys being recognized and worshiped as a god by the victim. Power plays an important role in satanic cults; as the Satanist rises in rank in the cult, he or she gradually surrenders the role of victim and takes on rights and privileges of a powerful god.

Where did Satanism begin? In an indirect form, the predecessors of Satanism may be found in archaic religions in which gods were worshipped, not because of their inherent goodness, but because of their perceived power. For example, the ancient Greek and Roman gods were such an amoral assemblage of deities. Few showed many admirable character traits. These gods were often depicted with all the foibles and venality of mere mortals. Many of the cults devoted to such gods and goddesses allegedly involved traumatizing rituals (e.g., the mystery cults). On the other hand, some religions specifically worshipped and supplicated overtly evil deities.

However, in some cases appearances may be deceiving. For example, the Yezidi sect of Turkey, Syria, Armenia, and Iran, worship Ahriman (who, in the Zoroastrian religion, is roughly the equivalent of Satan). However, the Yezidi believe that Ahriman is no longer evil, having asked for and having received God's forgiveness. They consider it an outrage to equate their Ahriman with the Satan of Christianity, and Islam.[1]

Worshipping evil

In other cases, what appears to be the worship of an "evil deity" may simply represent the worship of a spiritual entity who no longer enjoys favored status. There are examples in history in which a culture's demons were really past divinities, no longer revered, and sometimes given new and less attractive roles. Such revolutions among the gods sometimes resulted from conquests, whereupon the new gods of the conquerors take the place previously held by the gods of the conquered.

In other instances, evil may be revered or worshipped outright. In cultures in which Christianity is prevalent one might assume that the worship of evil would entail some devotion to Lucifer or Satan, the primary names given to the Euro-American spiritual representation of evil. To many traditional Christians, Satan and Lucifer are equivalent but different names for the same demon. However, many theologians make the distinction that Lucifer is the name of Satan before his fall. Within some occult traditions there is even a clearer discrimination between Satan and Lucifer. As already mentioned, within certain cults Lucifer is sometimes portrayed as a Promethean figure, the "bringer of light." In the tradition of some Gnostics, Lucifer is represented as the rebellious spirit opposed to Christianity and the god of creation who is instead portrayed as the one responsible for introducing evil by creating a material world. Thus, Luciferianism reverses the Judeo-Christian-Islamic concept of a good creator and an evil demon. Satan is occasionally presented in such relatively benign terms[2] but, more often, Satan is described as the personification of pure evil. Such a Satanic theology would attribute goodness to the Judeo-Christian God, but Satanists worship Satan because he is perceived to be more powerful or because the cultist might view himself or herself as being beyond redemption by a benign deity. In this system of thinking, goodness itself is characterized as a weak, ineffective, and futile goal. Spence describes a similar dichotomy in views of Satanism and Luciferianism although he defines his terms slightly differently:

> Modern groups practicing Satanism are small and obscure, and unorganized as they are, details concerning them are conspicuous by their absence. Plentiful details, however, are forthcoming concerning the cults of Lucifer, but much discrimination is required in dealing with these, the bulk of the literature on the subject being manifestly imaginative and willfully misleading. The members of the church of Lucifer are of two groups, those who regard the deity they adore as the evil principle, thus approximating to the standpoint of the Satanists, and those who look upon him as the true god in opposition to Adonai or Jehovah, whom they regard as an evil deity who has with fiendish ingenuity miscreated the world of man to the detriment of humanity. (1993, p. 123)

The wearing of dark, hooded robes is a commonly reported feature of these cults, but survivors describe a variety of different costumes and ritual acts. One patient arrived at my office with a ceremonial cowl.[3] When she brought it to me, neither she nor I knew what it was. Without identifying the patient to whom the item belonged, I asked other survivors if they recognized the article of clothing, and I was told that it was a cowl, a form of ceremonial headdress. The survivors indicated it was authentic, pointing to details of its construction that I had not even noticed. The patient who brought it to me reported that she had awakened from a trance in her own house. The cowl was on her head, but she did not know how or why it had gotten there. Some survivors describe the wearing of a miter by high-ranking members of their cult. The miter is a somewhat cone-shaped ceremonial hat worn by Catholic bishops and abbots. Some of the artwork from earlier times depicting the trial and execution of "heretics" by the Inquisition shows them dressed in miters and robes.

Simulated abuse and torture

Sexual abuse, torture,[4] and murder are often alleged to be important components of Satanic cult rituals. However, some of the survivors claim that rituals involving the torture or murder of a person can be simulated. In these cases, the simulation is conducted in a sufficiently realistic manner that many of the participants will believe that they witnessed the deliberate ceremonial killing of a person. In the Fran's Day Care criminal case, a child testified that he was told to close his eyes and that his perpetrator was cutting on his arm to perform surgery to replace his bone with the bone of Satan. However, the child revealed to the court that he unobtrusively peeked and saw that the "surgery" had not actually happened.

The predecessors of Satanism may be found in archaic religions in which gods were worshipped, not because of their inherent goodness, but because of their perceived power.

An adult patient described an abusive act she once observed in which a naked woman was tied to a chair in front of a table where a bloody razor blade was prominently displayed. The woman was then blindfolded, and the perpetrator took a straight pin and slowly ran it across the victim's body, causing slight scratches. According to my patient, the victim's reaction showed her terror—she believed she was being sliced with the razor blade, and consequently, she appeared to go in and out of numerous dissociated mental states.

Acts of ritual murder also are reportedly simulated for the purpose of terrorizing those present into silence and creating further states of dissociation. "Actual human sacrifice of children and adults may also be performed, but only on special occasions. Mock killings are performed more often and are designed to look as believable as real killings" (Smith, 1993, p. 130). Barb Jackson (1993), another survivor, describes her observations of an abusive cult in which abusive rituals actually occurred but also were sometimes simulated. Both reportedly had the capacity for being overwhelmingly traumatizing.[5]

Hearing countless reports of ritual abuse by patients and others, an obvious question arises: why would anyone want to *do* these things? The stories seemed to lack any redeeming features whatsoever. What would motivate people to carry out such practices? When asked, the patients sometimes have an answer to such questions. The most commonly given explanation is that such rituals provide an intoxicating sense of power to those who are in the role of perpetrating the abuse. Such a practitioner experiences the sense of power over life and death, either simulated or in actuality. During such abusive acts one exerts great control over the minds of the abused and dominion over the creation of what might appear to be new souls or, as one patient explained, "the souls of dead people," which can then "inhabit" the body of someone present at the ceremony. In actuality, these "souls" are more likely to be alternate or dissociated personalities created via traumatizing rituals.

Nevertheless, in such a role, the cultist not only "plays god," but for the purposes of those present, actually becomes the god (e.g., through a state of possession) and is recognized, respected, and worshipped as the god by the followers. On other occasions the cultist simply enjoys being in the powerful role of a god.[6] The following was written by one of my patients about such an interaction. According to the patient, an abusive male repetitively claimed he was God before sexually abusing her:

> Was taken into a room and thrown down on a bed. The man was very big and blonde. Muscular. Over 6 ft. tall. Very angular features. Had been "led" to the room by others. "He" told them to leave me alone with him. Said he was going to teach me a lesson. We talked back to him. He got right in my face and said he was God. He repeated it over and over. He kept saying he was God. "God. God. God." When we first were taken in to the room, we were scared. After he kept saying God, we were very compliant [sic].[7]

Another ritually abused patient sometimes switched to altered states, describing in tenor her experience of being tortured by "gods." But the gods she described were not metaphysical abstractions; they were merely people who had taken on the role or persona of gods in rituals she had been forced to attend. My patient called one of these "gods" Satan.[8]

The pursuit of power

The pursuit of power[9] may appear particularly attractive to those who have been coerced into conditions of extreme powerlessness, a feature of being in the victim role in such a cult. Apparently all, or almost all, members of Satanic cults reportedly are, at one time or another, in the victim roles of these abusive rituals. However, as one's rank increases in the cult, the extent of victimization decreases; thus as the cult member rises in power, he or she is increasingly placed in the role of a perpetrator of painful ceremonies and procedures.[10] Power can be desirable for its defensive as well as offensive potential. Getting power decreases the harm experienced by the individual. Sometimes the power of "the dark side" may be sought because the individual has lost any hope of protection from "good" people or a good deity. As one patient explained while in the state of a child alter, "God can't protect you. Satan can."

Several patients describe rituals in which Christian ceremonies are parodied and the victim of the abuse is told to pray to God for help. No help is forthcoming because the participants deliberately orchestrate the situation so that no aid can appear under such conditions. In some circumstances, no relief is offered until the victim makes a sincere plea to Satan or until the victim is transformed by the torture into another identity (through dissociation), one who is a devoted follower of Satan.

The most commonly given explanation is that [criminal] rituals provide an intoxicating sense of power to those who are in the role of perpetrating the abuse.

The power that exists in Satanic (and Luciferian) cults is reportedly reflected in an organized hierarchy with incremental ranks.[11] These positions may vary somewhat from one group to another, but one such hierarchy consists of: page, knight, priest (or priestess), prince (or princess), high priest (or high priestess), king (or queen), savior, and god (sometimes goddess, but goddess is not always the feminine equivalent of god and vice versa). As one increases in rank, one is taught more about the programming cues or "triggers" used in ceremonies with the other followers of the cult. Some of these triggers are relatively generic and thus can be used with a relatively large number of people. [One] example . . . is the repeated use of the word *deep* or *deeper*. When this word is used repeatedly, even unobtrusively, (e.g., in ordinary conversation) many survivors of Satanic and Luciferian cults will enter into a trance or show some other signs of change in mental state or other physical response such as an eyeblink or altered gaze.

Those who increase in rank are not only taught a variety of triggering stimuli that they can use in controlling others (via such programming methods), but they are also reportedly deprogrammed so that their responses to these lower-level generic cues are less powerful. Thus, survivors who are higher ranking in the Satanic (and similar) cults are "trained" with more highly specific and idiosyncratic programming cues so that the majority of other members will not readily have control over them. Such control remains with the elite, who are higher in rank and skill.

Notes

1. See Guest (1987).

2. For example, by Anton LaVey.

3. A cowl is a more tight-fitting hood-like article of apparel. The one brought to me was made of fabric that was somewhat stretchable and when it was worn it looked something like a ski mask with one opening exposing the wearer's two eyes.

4. See Golston (1992).

5. Dr. Harry Wright, a Philadelphia dentist, described witnessing what appeared to be the ritual sacrifice of a child in a jungle village in Brazil. Horrified he planned to leave the village the next day but found the girl in

question was unharmed. He implies that this was accomplished by slight of hand (1957).

6. Symonds, a biographer of Aleister Crowley, and one of the editors of Crowley's autobiography, *The Confessions of Aleister Crowley,* notes Crowley's conception of himself as a god (Symonds, 1979, p. 21).

7. Notice that the patient often uses the plural term "we" in making reference to herself. This is one of the frequently observed features of multiple personality disorder.

8. In some cases, perhaps many cases, the "gods" described by ritual abuse survivors may reflect not so much Satanism as other varieties of occultism.

9. Although some claim that there is actually a psychic or spiritual power to be achieved in such cults I have never observed any evidence of that. Instead the power that can be obtained is (1) the license to inflict harm on others during such ritual activities and (2) the opportunity to learn programming skills to influence or control others by using programming cues (often outside the context of the ritual activities).

10. E.g., see McShane (1993), p. 207.

11. Certain very high-ranking positions are held exclusively by certain individuals. However, in the tradition of some Gnostics (see Pagels, 1981) a variety of individuals may have some rotating role of relative importance (e.g., priestess or high priestess).

References

Golston, J.C. (1992). Ritual Abuse: Raising Hell in Psychotherapy. *Treaty Abuse Today,* 2(6), 5–16.

Gueste, J.S. (1987) *The Yezidis: A Study in Survival.* London: KPI.

Jackson, B. (1993, September). *The role of ritual abuse and the sexual exploitation of children.* Presented at the National Conference on Crimes Against Children, Washington, DC.

McShane, C. (1993). Satanic Sexual Abuse: A Paradigm. *Affilia,* 8, 200–212.

Pagels, E. (1981). *The Gnostic Gospels.* New York: Vintage Books.

Smith, M. (1993). *Ritual abuse: What it is, why it happens, how to help.* San Francisco: HarperSanFrancisco.

Spence, L. (1993). *An encyclopedia of occultism.* New York: Carol Publishing.

Symonds, J., and Grant, K. (Eds.). (1979) *The Confessions of Alelster Crowley.* London: Arkana.

3

Satanic Ritual Abuse
Is a Serious Problem

Gordan A. Magill

Gordan A. Magill is a survivor of satanic ritual abuse and a freelance writer.

Satanic ritual abuse (SRA) is a serious problem in the United States; however, the victims' claims of SRA are dismissed by many as hoaxes or a form of mass hysteria. Those who advocate the "mass hysteria" theory refuse to accept firsthand accounts of abuse by the children or adults who were victimized because they claim their memories are unreliable. The only eyewitness testimony that mass hysteria theorists would believe is that of former Satanists; however, since the mass hysteria believers refuse to accept the existence of Satanists, not even their testimony would be believed. Simply because the victims of SRA do not give specific facts about their abuse does not mean that no abuse occurred. Satanic ritual abuse has many similarities to organized crime and it must be investigated in much the same way organized crime is.

> The real issue isn't whether or not children's stories of ritual sex abuse are honest accounts or lies, but whether or not the stories are verifiable. We need only recall that the original charges of witchcraft in Salem were made by young girls who were carried away by group hysteria. (*Satanic Panic*, p. 111)[1]

The specter of the Salem witch hunts loom over American society like the grim reaper lifting his sickle of death. Accusations of witch hunts seem to appear in our media everyday—especially when someone is accused of child abuse, or occult crime. The mere mention of witch hunt conjures images of mass hysteria, which overshadows all facts, and slays all hope for an honest debate or investigation. Anyone who is accused of fueling this mass hysteria is stigmatized with the label of witch hunter, and this alone is deemed sufficient reason to dismiss all their evidence and arguments, no matter how compelling. What we have in America today is hysteria over hysteria.

Reprinted, with permission, from "Hysteria over Hysteria: Specter of the Salem Witch Hunts," by Gordon A. Magill, Web article at http://members.aol.com/dovelion/ritual/hysteria.htm. Copyright 1998 by Gordon A. Magill.

19

Jeffrey S. Victor in his book *Satanic Panic* says:

> Dangerous, criminal Satanists and Satanic cults are an in-
> vented internal enemy. This . . . belief . . . brings together
> some fundamentalist Protestants and conservative Catholics
> who have been long-lasting conflicting parties over many is-
> sues in American society. It joins them with some secular
> child advocates and feminists, with whom religious tradi-
> tionalists are currently in conflict over a wide range of fam-
> ily issues. It joins many secular police officers, social workers,
> and psychotherapists together with some Christian funda-
> mentalist evangelists, groups which normally would be a bit
> distrustful of each other's credibility and authority. (Pages
> 200–203)[1]

Jeffrey S. Victor tells us it is not Satanists and child abusers we need
to fear. It is fundamentalists, feminists, police officers, social workers, and
psychotherapists who are "inventing" devils, "scapegoating," perpetrating a dangerous "hoax," and projecting their own fearful "fantasies" on
society. Never mind that the agreement between "long-lasting conflicting
parties" is a strong argument that there is occult crime. Never mind that
the source of agreement between these "long lasting conflicting parties"
is that they help people. The reasoning goes something like this:

> There are no devils and there are no devil worshippers
> therefore what we are to fear are the people who report Sa-
> tanic crimes. Sure there are insane people who think they
> are devil worshippers; sure there are a few social deviants
> who use Satanism as an excuse to fulfill their deviant de-
> sires; sure there are a few kids experimenting with Satanism
> (probably because they are rebelling against some funda-
> mentalist who gave them the idea in the first place); but
> there are no devils; so there are no devil worshippers; and
> there is no such thing as ritual abuse. Therefore, it is not Sa-
> tanists we need to fear—what we need to fear is mass hyste-
> ria and those who spread it.

Hard to believe

I admit that the thought of Satan worshippers abusing and murdering
children is hard to believe, because it is outside the range of "normal" human experience. The Holocaust was hard to believe, because it was outside the range of "normal" human experience. The news that the nice
neighbor next door slaughtered and cannibalized young boys is hard to
believe, because it is outside the range of "normal" human experience.
But this idea that the insane, deviant, and immature worship Satan in a
vacuum, and that a wide cross section of helping professionals are spreading false rumors and fueling mass hysteria is hard to believe, because it is
so unreasonable. If there was not an extremely vocal minority with impressive titles and degrees aggressively promoting this idea of a mass hysteria, it would be summarily dismissed. The degrees and titles of those
who warn us that Satanic ritual abuse is happening in America are per-

haps even more impressive. But somehow, either because of the aggressiveness of the mass hysteria proponents, or the attentiveness of the news media, the mass hysteria hypothesis has been accepted by many. There may be another reason for this acceptance.

It may be that the advocates for victims of ritual abuse acknowledge their bias and are committed to fair debate, while there are proponents of mass hysteria whose sole commitment is to accomplish their hidden agenda. The very meaning of the word occult is "hidden." Ritual abuse occurs in secret and those who commit this abuse do so in secret. Some who do so hold "responsible," "respectable," positions in society, and make decisions and take action based on their hidden agenda without stating their real reasons. Like the pedophile who asserts that he did not abuse or harm a child, because he redefines sexual contact with a child as love, the Satanist redefines ritual child abuse and murder as mass hysteria. I am not saying every proponent of mass hysteria is a pedophile or Satanist, but I am saying that some are aggressively fanning the flames of hysteria because they have hidden agendas. The question now is, how are we to ensure that those who redefine and distort facts are exposed.

The thought of Satan worshippers abusing and murdering children is hard to believe, because it is outside the range of "normal" human experience. The Holocaust was hard to believe.

This should be a concern for honest proponents of mass hysteria as well as a concern for advocates of ritual abuse victims. We either have people with hidden "right wing agendas" on one side, or people with hidden "subversive agendas" on the other side. The only way to eliminate hidden agendas from the public debate is to verify the facts. That seems to be what Jeffrey S. Victor is calling for in the opening quote for this viewpoint. That seems to be what proponents of mass hysteria are calling for when they ask where the evidence is. Well, if that is what they are really calling for, then why don't they call for the government to take the necessary steps to verify the evidence.

Remember, ritual abuse is occult in nature, and the nature of the occult, just like the nature of child abuse, is that it is hidden and secret. Sometimes it sounds like the only evidence acceptable to the proponents of mass hysteria is photographs and videos, or fairly fresh bodies. Proponents of mass hysteria say children cannot be believed because they are not reliable witnesses. Adults who tell of ritual abuse cannot be believed because they are mentally ill, or have recovered memories which cannot be trusted. The police cannot infiltrate occult groups because they might infringe on their religious liberties. Therefore, according to proponents of mass hysteria there can be no eyewitness testimony unless it is from a practicing Satanist who successfully breaks from the group; and since there is no such thing as a practicing Satanist anyone that makes such a claim is a liar. Never mind that there are ways to determine if a child's testimony is true; never mind that there are ways to determine if recovered memories are true. Never mind that the purpose of the judicial system is to determine the whole truth. "Show us the hard evidence!" demands the proponents of mass hysteria, but do they really care about the evidence?

Hidden evidence

Matamoras, New Mexico, is one case where there were bodies and evidence of occult rituals, but the proponents of mass hysteria say that like every other case where there is hard evidence, it is the exception that proves the rule. Photographs depicting child pornography and bestiality were found in the Franklin murder case, and while that seems to go to motive, they are deemed irrelevant by proponents of mass hysteria. Do the proponents really care about evidence or do they only care about their own hidden agenda? Do they care about protecting children or do they care about protecting pedophiles? Do they care about protecting children or do they care about protecting Satanists? If they care about the evidence then they should call for the kind of investigation necessary to determine if evidence of occult crime exists.

Ritual abuse is occult in nature, and the nature of the occult, just like the nature of child abuse, is that it is hidden and secret.

Children who were abused by occult groups cannot be expected to know who was murdered and what was done with the bodies. Adults who recover memories of ritual childhood abuse were victims, not perpetrators. They were not privy to the secrets of the group. In many cases victims of ritual abuse know they traveled long distances, but do not know where the crime occurred. This does not mean there was no abuse. This does not mean there were no murders. The issue is not, as Victor says, "whether or not the stories are verifiable." The issue is, did ritual abuse occur? And the only way to verify this is to treat ritual abuse like organized crime. Occult crime is hidden and it must be uncovered. Occult crime is organized (the occult emphasis on individual autonomy may make one central authority unlikely but there are many organized groups) and a nationally organized investigation must be conducted. Occult crime poses unique problems as members of the group are required to participate in unlawful drug use and depraved sexual acts. Occult crime has a spiritual belief system which must be understood and confronted within the bounds of the Constitution. Any call for evidence which does not call for steps such as these is mere polemic. The reports that are coming in of occult crime throughout our country demand that these steps be taken. The country cannot remain in a state of charges and counter charges of: ritual crime and mass hysteria; recovered memories and false allegations; occult conspiracies and right wing conspiracies. We must determine who is being deprived of the justice that our Constitution promises to all.

We need to learn from history. The few who warned that Hitler must be stopped were labeled warmongers and fear mongers. Their reports were unsettling but they were true, and the consequences of ignoring their reports permittted unimaginable death and destruction. The proponents of mass hysteria ignore history and label anyone who warns us of unimaginable and unsettling crimes a rumor monger or conspirator. The proponents of mass hysteria ignore the history of the Salem witch hunts and label those who report occult crimes as witch hunters, but there is no comparison between the Salem witch hunts and reports of ritual abuse. When the Salem witch hunts occurred there was no United States of America; there was no Constitution; the government was in a state of transition and the governor was absent; the church was also in a state of transition; but even then the church and government themselves ended the excesses that were occurring. Today we have a Constitution, an established government, and past experiences to guide us in how to prosecute occult crime without depriving people of religious liberty. Today we have sophisticated investigative techniques and effective psychological methods to determine truth from lies. So stop the polemic about "Where is the evidence?" Stop this spreading of hysteria over hysteria. Join with the helping professionals who are reporting ritual crimes, and urge the government to take the necessary steps to determine what evidence exists.

Reference

1. Jeffrey S. Victor, *Satanic Panic: The Creation of a Contemporary Legend.* Chicago: Open Court, 1993.

4

Church of Satan's Advice to Youth

Church of Satan

The Church of Satan was founded by Anton Szandor LaVey on April 30, 1966. It is the oldest and largest organized satanic religion.

Questions commonly asked by teens about Satanism are answered. There is no standard for what a Satanist is supposed to be like; the only requirement to be a Satanist is to live like one. Although members must be eighteen to officially join the Church of Satan, Satanists of any age can practice the rituals and explore the Dark Realm.

D ue to the ever-increasing amount of mail that we have received from young people who are new to Satanism, we feel the time has come to put together some information to help answer your specific questions and concerns.

If you have read our books, you know that Satanism isn't about taking drugs, and it isn't about harming animals or children. Unlike many religions and philosophies, Satanism respects and exalts life. Children and animals are the purest expressions of that life force, and as such are held sacred and precious in the eyes of the Satanist. Besides, it is very un-Satanic to take any creature's life against its will. It is equally un-Satanic to cloud your brain and impair your judgment with mind-altering substances. A real magician has no need of those kinds of things, as he should be able to bring about changes in consciousness by the very power of his Will and imagination.

If you have not yet read *The Satanic Bible*, you should do so. It has a lot more information on our attitude toward Satan, and will give you a clearer idea of our philosophy, ideals and goals. Perhaps at first they will be difficult for you to understand, because you may have been raised in an environment that dictates that God=Good and Satan=Evil. The truth is that good and evil are often terms that people twist to suit their own purposes. Sometimes people will lie and try to make you think certain things just so you will do what they want you to do. Always remember

Reprinted, with permission, from "Church of Satan Youth Communiqué," at www.churchofsatan.com/Pages/Youthletter.html.

that the final judgment is yours. That is both a great freedom and a great responsibility. For us, Satan is a symbol of the power of that choice.

There is no one way that a Satanist is "supposed" to be. Uniqueness and creativity are encouraged here, not mindless conformity. It doesn't matter what kind of music you like to listen to; it doesn't make any difference whether you prefer gothic music, black metal music, classical music, old popular tunes, or show tunes. It doesn't matter what style of clothes you like to wear. What *does* matter is that you are a mature, sensitive, self-aware individualist who revels in the Darkness, and who wishes to align yourself with others who share your views. In this world of prefabricated, media-saturated, unoriginal drones, it is up to the Satanist to cherish, maintain, and preserve *true* individuality and creativity. Satan represents freedom from hypocrisy, from convenient lies, and challenges that which is presumed to be true. He is strong and defiant, and inspires us to our own strengths.

Frequently asked questions

That said, let's address some of your most commonly asked questions:

"How old do I have to be to join the Church of Satan?"

You may become a member of the Church of Satan at any age, though further participation in the organization is limited to those who are eighteen years of age or older. This is not meant as a judgment of your maturity; we've received letters from 14-year-olds who had a distinct, mature grasp of Satanism. But we must be realistic about the world around us. One reason is that we don't want to become a haven for the kind of sanctimonious perverts that Christian churches and other "Goodguy Badge" forums (such as Big Brother/Big Sister, Boy Scouts, etc.) often are. There are a lot of sick people out there, and we don't want our vital young Satanists to become victims of twisted adults who are more interested in contacting young kids than they are in practicing Satanism.

Another reason is because your parents or other adults in your life may not understand or might be hostile toward your exploration of this religion. They may try to cause trouble for us, falsely accusing us of any number of things, just because they feel threatened. So, we simply cannot allow anyone under the legal age of consent to participate in any activities directly sponsored by the Church of Satan. The *only* exception to this rule would be with the *written permission and attendance* of your parent or legal guardian. Some of you may be lucky enough to have a very good relationship with your parents and they may be supportive, even enthusiastic, about your exploration of the Dark Side. They may be willing to go with you to meet a local Grotto Master and decide on your level of participation at this point in your magical development. If this is the case, let us know.

"Do I have to become a member to be a 'real' Satanist?"

All you have to do to be a real Satanist is start living like one. Dr. LaVey wrote *The Satanic Bible* so that people could pick up a copy, read it, and know everything they need to know about Satanism and how to put it to work in their own lives. Most people who choose to become members do so as a symbolic act to themselves, to formally align themselves with others of like mind, and to show their support for a philosophy and way of life they agree with. It is a purely personal decision—we don't solicit memberships. But actual membership usually conveys to others that you are serious about your beliefs, and that you know enough about it to have read Dr. LaVey's works and align yourself with his spearhead organization. It usually grants you a certain amount of respect as an authority. If you were going to speak as a member of the Church in a public forum, you should actually be one. If you were going to start a grotto affiliated with the Church of Satan, you'd have to be a member (again, you'd have to be over the age of eighteen). But as far as benefiting from Satanism in your life, or defending true Satanism, those are the rights and responsibilities of every Satanist, "official" or not.

"My parents and friends don't understand me, and don't approve of my interest in Satanism. How can I make them accept my beliefs, and where can I go to perform my rituals?"

Unfortunately, most young Satanists face this problem. Few of us are lucky enough to have sympathetic parents, or others around like ourselves. However, as long as you are living under your parents' roof and they are feeding and taking care of you, you do owe them a degree of consideration. Offer to let them read your books, and talk about what misunderstandings they may have from T.V. talk shows and Christian propaganda. But you can't force anyone to understand what, for you, is an obvious and magical revelation. If Satanism offends others who have necessary control over your life right now, do your studies and rituals in private. If you don't have a place at home where you can be alone, find a special spot on the beach, in a field, or in the woods where you can ritualize when you need to. While you are understandably enthusiastic about your new-found religion, it is not very Satanic to make yourself miserable by creating a problem with your parents when you have to live in the same house together, or at school where your real goal may be to aggravate those in authority in the guise of "expressing your individuality."

Satanism isn't about taking drugs, and it isn't about harming animals or children.

Practice Lesser Magic. Remember that a competent Satanic magician should be able to size up any situation and weigh his choices of action to bring about desired results. Enthusiasm is certainly encouraged and appreciated, however Satanism asks no one to be a martyr. And keep in mind that most people simply aren't going to understand because, ultimately, they don't want to. That is as it should be. Satanism is not for everyone. Satan, by his very nature, walks alone. He is the true individualist, the outcast. This doesn't mean that you cannot care about those who are close to you; Satan also represents love, kindness and respect to those who deserve it. It just means that you should not concern yourself with people who do not approve of you. Revel in your uniqueness; be proud of who and what you are. Achieve all you can with the strength and determination of Satan himself coursing proudly through your veins. When Satanism leads to positive changes in your accomplishments and attitude, your parents and other adults around you will notice. The best way you can represent Satanism is by providing a living example of how the diabolical arts have made you a stronger, more focused person. The results will speak louder than any logical argument you can present.

"Is it better to study and ritualize alone, or to work with others?"

Unless you are able to find others who are as knowledgeable about Satanism as you are, it is better to work alone. If you do choose to ritualize with others, you must make certain that they are 100% clear on what Satanism is all about. If they are into it just out of curiosity or for thrills, they'll get their thrills all right—the wrong kind! Many young Satanists find they have one close, magical friend who they feel they can work with, but usually one of you is actually magically stronger and more sincere, and chances are that's *you*, since you're the one who has gone through the trouble of actually contacting the Church of Satan. It's often best for you to work and study alone, guided by the material in our literature, rather than have your magic and concentration diluted by would-be friends. As the saying goes, a chain is only as strong as its weakest link. What that means in this case is that if you perform rituals with others who are not as serious and dedicated as you are, they will hinder your magic, not strengthen it. Many adult Satanists work and study alone by choice. Finding a *true* magical partner can be stimulating and rewarding, but if you need such a person in your magical progression, you'll conjure one up (see Herman Hesse's *Demian* or *Illusions* by Richard Bach).

Satan also represents love, kindness and respect to those who deserve it.

Don't be disturbed or frightened or think you're crazy when you feel contacted by the Dark Ones you conjure forth, or by the magical results you begin to produce. You're not crazy for feeling the way you do about the hypocrisy, blindness and incompetence you see all around you. Nor are you crazy to see the results of your Black Magic. Approach the Dark Masters with the proper degree of respect and decorum—that's what rituals are for, to establish a relationship. If you approach the demons respectfully, they will reward you with knowledge, guidance, and success. Your demon guide is within *you*—don't look for it outside. You just have to contact that part of yourself and listen to it. That is the most important work anyone can do.

"Do I need all the things mentioned in The Satanic Bible *to do my rituals?"*

You don't need everything mentioned in Dr. LaVey's books to do an effective ritual. Maybe you don't have the money to obtain, or the private space to store, items such as swords, chalices, black robes, gongs and elaborate altars. Here is a powerful ritual you can perform tonight, and all you need is a quiet place where you can be alone, a Baphomet either on your person or in front of you, and a single black candle:

> Light the candle and set it before you. Sit up straight, breathe deeply and relax. Clear your mind of all outside thoughts. As you gaze at the flame, say in your mind or out loud, "I am ready, oh, Dark Lord. I feel your strength within me and wish to honor you in my life. I am one of the Dev-

il's Own. Hail Satan!" Open your mind. It will take time. You may think you are ready, but you may still find you cannot let go right away. Concentrate on your image of Satan and on the word "strength" and listen to what comes up from yourself. You have answers for yourself that no one else can give you. This is a simple way of conjuring Satan into your life. He'll snap you into line and tell you what you have to do to be happy, strong and focused—and he'll give you the stamina and courage to push yourself to do it. The path you've chosen won't be easy; sometimes it may be a nightmare. But when you are ready to face the challenge, it will be there.

A few final words

A few final words: Just because you are not yet eighteen doesn't mean that you cannot explore on your own these Dark Realms that are opening before you. This is a very potent, magical time. You were compelled to write to us for a reason, and right now you are going through an initiation into the Black Arts that must be all your own. Your body and your mind are going through intense changes. Take this time to learn all you can—about yourself and about the world around you. Explore your skills, talents, and inventiveness. Learn to play music, paint or build a robot. Use your brain and your heart to find out what is right, what is true, and what will make you stronger. You are not alone. You are different; you are superior, and it's okay for you to feel that way. You see what others do not; you know what evil lurks in the hearts of men. *Don't* settle for white-light bullshit just because you can't actively participate with other "official" Satanists right now. Don't fill your mind and dilute your magic with crap. Don't believe someone who claims to know more about Satanism than you do. You're the one who contacted us; you might even join. A friend your age probably doesn't know nearly as much about real magic as you do. An adult who claims special powers and who says he can initiate you into the Dark Realms is probably just looking to fuel his own ego (or wallet).

Read our *Bunco Sheet* carefully so that you won't be taken advantage of, and look over the rest of our information. You don't have to join. Remember, to be a true Satanist all you have to do is start living like one, so don't complicate your life by pushing when it isn't necessary. Your status within the Church of Satan will be based on your real accomplishments in the outside world, not how many magical sigils you've memorized. The Church of Satan will be here when you are ready, and if your commitment is strong and sincere, you will benefit from this time. Your family and friends might be concerned at first because they've been brainwashed about what Satanism is. If they love you, when they see the positive changes that occur due to your new dedication to Satanism (and most of all, to yourself) they'll try to understand and support you.

Best wishes for further success and fulfillment. You are with us.

HAIL SATAN!

5

Anti-Satanism Is Bigotry

Michael J. Mazza

Michael J. Mazza is a Ph. D. student and teaching fellow in the Department of English at the University of Pittsburgh. He is also a veteran of the U.S. Naval Reserve and currently serves as an officer in the U.S. Army Reserve.

Satanism is a legitimate, but misunderstood, religion. Its members are law-abiding and serious about their religion. Nevertheless, Satanists have been subjected to mean-spirited—and fraudulent—propaganda based on the actions of a few misguided youth. Most Satanists are free-thinking rebels who make valuable contributions to society by encouraging others to rethink old prejudices and preconceptions.

On today's diverse college campus, people do a lot of educating about various forms of bigotry. Racism, sexism, anti-Semitism—these and other irrational forms of prejudice are rightly opposed by people of conscience.

At the risk of sounding "politically correct," I would like to take the opportunity to expose and denounce one of the last acceptable forms of bigotry in our "enlightened" culture.

I'm talking about anti-Satanism.

A legitimate religion

It might surprise some people to find out that Satanism is just as legitimate a religion as any other in the world today. Modern Satanism was essentially founded by the late Anton Szandor LaVey, whose classic work *The Satanic Bible* has been in print since its first publication in 1969. Like any religious movement, LaVey's original Church of Satan www.churchofsatan.com has spawned a number of offshoots, including the Temple of Set www.xeper.org, the First Church of Satan www.firstchurchofsatan.org, and the Sinagogue of Satan www.zoo-gate.fi/~lvythn/sos/.

Research and educational foundations such as the Australian Satanic Council www.satanic.org.au also help educate the general public about this misunderstood faith.

I have corresponded and spoken with Satanists all over the world, and found them to be a diverse and interesting group of individuals. Most of them are hard-working, law-abiding people who are as serious about their religion as are members of any "mainstream" church. They are opposed to animal sacrifices and other harmful activities.

Nevertheless, Satanists have been subjected to inaccurate and mean-spirited propaganda since the establishment of the modern religion three decades ago.

Typical of this anti-Satanic nonsense is Tipper Gore's 1987 book *Raising PG Kids in an X-Rated Society*. In this book Mrs. Gore calls Satanism a "cancer" upon society.

Mrs. Gore's book contributed to the so-called "Satanic panic" of the 1980s. During this time sensational TV shows aired alleged "exposés" of Satanic cult abuses

However, most of the anti-Satanic accusations were totally fraudulent. Professor Jeffrey S. Victor, a sociologist in the State University of New York system, has devastatingly exposed the anti-Satanic sham in his meticulously documented 1993 book *Satanic Panic*.

Despite Victor's work, many today are trying to keep the Satanic panic alive.

Satanism is just as legitimate a religion as any other in the world today.

Yes, some misguided teenagers are going to incorporate "Satanic" symbology into their criminal activities. But these kids clearly haven't taken the time to really read *The Satanic Bible*. And do we label it a "Christian ritual crime" when Baptist or Catholic youth break the law? There seems to be a double standard here.

The sad fact is that Satanist-bashers can make money with their bigotry. Lots of naive dupes are willing to give greedy evangelists money to fight the "Satanic agenda." And Christian bookstores continue to sell anti-Satanic propaganda.

It's no wonder that the *Satanic Bible* proclaims, "Satan has been the best friend the church has ever had, as he has kept it in business all these years!"

As I said before, Satanists are a pretty diverse group, and it's hard to make generalizations about their beliefs and practices. Many, if not most, don't even view Satan as a real being; rather, he is seen as an empowering symbol.

One common denominator I have found among Satanists is a refusal to let themselves be controlled or intimidated by the pulpit-pounders of "mainstream" churches.

Satanists are often iconoclastic, free-thinking religious rebels. And most of them are also creative, life-loving people who have something of value to offer society.

The Australian Satanic Council, for example, has been at the forefront of the battle against internet censorship. When Satanists like these fight for freedom of speech, we all benefit.

But more than that, Satanism challenges those of us who were raised in "mainstream" churches to rethink our old prejudices and preconceptions.

As Anton LaVey's *Satanic Bible* declares, "Satan represents undefiled wisdom, instead of hypocritical self-deceit!" Surely that's something we should all strive for, regardless of our own theological orientation.

Unfortunately, too many people are more interested in bashing other people's religion than in truly seeking after wisdom.

6

The Extent of Satanic Crime Is Exaggerated

Jeffrey S. Victor

Jeffrey S. Victor is a professor of sociology at State University of New York. He is the author of Satanic Panic: The Creation of a Contemporary Legend.

Claims about teen involvement in satanic cult activity are widely disseminated but are generally misinterpreted. Graffiti, cemetery vandalism, and sites mistaken as satanic altars are usually remnants of adolescent legend trips, a form of recreational entertainment in which teens test local legends about haunted sites or paranormal phenomena. When teens see the effect these innocent symbols have on adults who believe them to be evidence of satanic cults, many teens deliberately encourage such beliefs by acting out a parody of satanic cult activities. Other so-called occult-related crime is primarily petty juvenile crime by pseudo-Satanists who are self-taught from friends, books, heavy metal music, movies, and magazines. Almost all self-identified teen Satanists lack any elaborate belief system that is focused on devil worship. Instead, they use Satanism as a convenient excuse for their delinquent, aggressive, or rebellious behavior.

> *I and the public know*
> *What all schoolchildren learn,*
> *Those to whom evil is done*
> *Do evil in return.*
>
> W.H. Auden[1]

Claims about teenage Satanism

Perhaps the most widely accepted claims about Satanism are claims about *teenage* involvement in Satanic cult activity. These claims are being disseminated across the country by various groups which are concerned about teenagers and their possible involvement in crime. Local police spread claims about teenage ritualistic crime in police conferences, in lectures to community groups, and in police magazines. Child protection social workers spread the claims in conferences about the problems of youth. Anti-cult organizations spread the claims at conferences about teenage involvement in religious cults. A host of religious evangelists spread the claims at church and community meetings about teenage Satanism.

The particular claims vary, but there are many consistent assertions. Teenagers are generally said to be drawn gradually into an interest in occult ritual activity through a prior interest in heavy metal rock music, *Dungeons and Dragons* fantasy games, and books on occult magic. Some claims-makers also assert that secretive adult Satanists encourage these teenagers into deeper involvement in black magic ritualism and Satanic beliefs. It is commonly asserted that once teenagers become obsessed with Satanic magic and Devil worship, they are driven to commit increasingly serious anti-social acts, such as abusing drugs, vandalizing churches and cemeteries, and killing animals in ritual sacrifices. It is also commonly claimed that some of these teenage Satanists become so disturbed that they commit suicide and even murder. Some claims-makers assert that adult Satanists recruit new members into their secret criminal organizations from among teenagers in these "Satanic cults."

In her book, *The Devil's Web*, Pat Pulling, for example, offers a brief synopsis of these claims about teenage Satanism.

> Law enforcement officials and mental health professionals now recognize the fact that adolescent occult involvement is progressive. The child who is obsessed with occult entertainment may not stop there, but he often moves on to satanic graffiti and cemetery vandalism. From that point, he easily moves into grave robbing for items needed for occult rituals, and he is just a step away from blood-letting. Blood-letting begins with animal killings and mutilations and progresses to murder if intervention does not take place.[2]

Some claims-makers have developed elaborate explanations of stages and types of teenage Satanism; all are constructed without any basis in systematic empirical research data. In a police magazine, Dr. Ronald Holmes, a professor of criminal justice at the University of Louisville, for example, offers a scheme for identifying the progressive involvement of teenagers in Satanism. While he admits in the article that there exists little reliable knowledge about the matter, he nevertheless fabricates an elaborate description of the stages of teenage Satanism. His underlying assumption is that teenagers learn Satanism much like someone learns a strange new religion.

Stage 1. The youth in the occult is immediately drawn into the world of black magic and the worship of the devil because he is told that great worldly power and temporary glory will be his for the asking. . . .

Stage 2. In this second stage, the initiate is now exposed to Satanic philosophies and becomes one with the demonic belief system. . . . This new member learns the prayers, spells, doctrines, dogmas of the faith, holidays, rituals, and the importance of being baptized in the blood of Satan. . . .

Stage 3. Now that the youth has progressed into the world of the Satanic, he is now accepted into the secret and religious ceremonies of the coven. He learns the various sabbats and the reasons for their celebrations. He participates in the sacrifice for Lucifer. . . . The Satanist at this level of participation and sophistication with the occult understands the proper animals for sacrifice. . . .

One sacrifice that the new member into Satanism may become involved with is the human sacrifice. At this stage the member becomes acutely aware that humans are indeed sacrificed for the devil, and the form of sacrifice will take two forms: blood or fire. . . .

Stage 4. In the final stage of total involvement in Satanism, the young person becomes firmly committed to the occult lifestyle. . . .

In the sabbats, the initiate is intimately involved in sexual orgies which are often an integral part of the worship ceremonies. Obviously, for the seriously disenfranchised members of the youth subculture, this can be a powerful drawing force into full membership.[3]

Teenage Satanism is linked to the secret Satanic cult conspiracy theory by claims that adults from secret Satanic groups operate as the guiding hand behind this indoctrination into Satanism. In this way, claims about teenage Satanism are incorporated into the broader Satanic cult legend, and given apparent credibility with other atrocity claims about ritual child abuse, missing children, ritual child sacrifice, and serial murder. The president of the Cult Awareness Council of Houston, Texas, for example, was quoted in a professional journal about family related violence, as making these claims at a seminar concerned with ritual child abuse and teenage Satanism.[4] According to the report about the seminar, she claimed that:

> Adult Satanists . . . provide an abandoned house for recruits where they engage in drugs, and sex, and listen to allegedly satanic, "heavy metal" music. . . . Initially, this is fun for the adolescents. Then, over time, and often while under the influence of some drugs, the recruits are encouraged to engage in various sexual behaviors. While the adolescents are engaging in sexual behaviors, and often unbeknownst to them, tapes of their activities are made. These tapes can be marketed as pornography, or they can be used to threaten or blackmail the adolescents into staying with the cult.[5]

When the average parent reads such assertions in local newspaper reports about teenage cemetery vandalism or animal mutilation, especially when the claims are made by so-called "experts" in teenage Satanism, they can easily be moved to fear that there is some grain of truth in the claims. Then, when they see strange symbolic graffiti on walls in their town, and teenagers in strange clothing displaying some of the same symbols, they can easily conclude that there is an epidemic of teenagers becoming involved in another new bizarre form of anti-social aggression, perhaps under the influence of adult, organized criminals.

Teenage behavior labelled as Satanism

There is an alternative way of understanding the meanings of teenage behavior mistakenly labelled as Satanism. If we put to use reliable research about teenage behavior, we can see that what gets labelled "Satanic activity" by the claims-makers is a diverse collection of activities, including adolescent legend trips, teenage fad behavior, malicious teenage delinquency, and pseudo-Satanism among groups of psychologically disturbed adolescents. When these diverse activities are lumped together and viewed through the distorting lens of belief in the Satanic cult legend, they are misinterpreted as evidence of teenage Satanism. Teenagers engaged in these activities do not constitute a cult or a religion, any more than a motorcycle gang constitutes a cult or the hippie counterculture a religion.

Adolescent legend trips

The graffiti, cemetery vandalism, and "altar" sites usually mistaken for evidence of teenage Satanism are most often simply remnants of adolescent legend trips. Research about this widely practiced teenage custom can be found in the writings of folklore scholars, particularly in the work of Bill Ellis.[6] Few psychologists or sociologists have studied the activity, perhaps because the behavior has been treated as unimportant pranks of rural and small town teenagers.

Contemporary folklore research has adopted the systematic methods of behavioral scientists to investigate orally transmitted traditions, such as children's games and stories, superstitions, proverbs and riddles, local legends, and recurrent rumor stories called "urban legends."[7] Folklore research is no longer the mere collection of quaint old tales and ancient myths. Some folklore scholars have turned their attention to the orally transmitted customs of adolescents, which they have investigated much like anthropologists doing field studies of tribal peoples.

The graffiti, cemetery vandalism, and "altar" sites usually mistaken for evidence of teenage Satanism are most often simply remnants of adolescent legend trips.

An adolescent legend trip involves the testing of a local legend about a scary supernatural site or paranormal incident.[8] The local legend may focus upon a supposedly haunted house or cemetery, or a site supposedly frequented by a witch. Often, parts of a local legend are used like a script for a re-enacted performance of the legend; for example, the legend might be about a ghost called up from the dead, or a witch's ritual in the woods. Legend trips are in some ways similar to the ghost stories told and acted out around campfires during evenings at summer camp.

A legend trip is a form of recreational entertainment. Even when magic spells are chanted or rituals performed, as they often are, the behavior is not an expression of any genuine belief in supernatural or paranormal powers. It is not in any way a religious practice. Instead, a legend trip, in order to be enjoyed, requires merely the temporary suspension of disbelief. This is much like what happens when people watch a supernatural horror movie in order to be frightened and amused. Too much skepticism and critical thinking makes the experience seem a bit ridiculous.

There are a great variety of these local supernatural legends. Bill Ellis offers a summary of some themes.

> Babies are especially popular victims of the accidents or murders that provide the background for legend-trips. They are often associated with a "Cry Baby Bridge," where their mothers murdered them or where they were flung out the window of a crashing car into the path of an oncoming lo-comotive. Decapitated ghosts, usually looking for their lost heads, also show up frequently. The headless horseman still rides near Cincinnati, but near Sandusky, Ohio, he has be-come a headless motorcycle man, his head cut off by piano wire stretched across the road, and near Cleveland the ghost is a headless little old lady in a Yellow Volkswagen. Headless women are twice as popular as headless men, and usually prowl bridges where they died in crashes or were murdered.[9]

A legend trip is a clandestine group activity, in which the presence of any adult is definitely not desired. One reason is that a legend trip functions as a kind of ritual for adolescents to prove their courage, much like some Indian adolescents used to prove their bravery by stealing horses from an-other Indian tribe.[10] Another reason is that a legend trip usually involves deliberately transgressing the rules of adult society and even breaking laws, in order to enhance the exciting risk of danger.[11] Adolescent legend trips are usually designed to shock and offend adult sensibilities. They are a way of "playing chicken," so that adolescents can test their anxieties about challenging adult authority. In a sense, adults are the other "tribe" for teenagers on a legend trip.

Legend trips and juvenile delinquency

Adolescent legend trips sometimes, but not always, involve such crimes as trespassing on private property, defacing property with graffiti, van-dalism, underage drinking, and in more recent years, the use of illegal drugs. Sexual activity may also occur, when boys make use of the fright-ening situation to provoke girls' desires for closer contact. This may some-times be a hidden agenda when boys bring their girlfriends along on a legend trip.

Teenagers who take part in legend trips, however, are usually not ha-bitual delinquents. They don't normally pursue a criminal life-style of ag-gressive, anti-social behavior. The crimes which may take place during legend trips are used to heighten tension. Breaking adult rules is part of the scripting of an exciting legend trip, rather than an expression of the supposed anti-social personalities of a few adolescents.

The research on adolescent legend trips indicates that these activities occur across the country. There are thousands of local legends about su-pernatural or paranormal happenings.[12] In Ohio alone, for example, 175 locations of legend trips have been identified by folklore researchers.[13] They occur in rural, small town, and suburban areas. (These are also the areas where almost all incidents of so-called teenage Satanism are re-ported in local newspapers.) The age level of teenagers involved in legend trips, according to the research, tends to be between twelve and eighteen, with participants more likely to be in their later teens.[14] There are no records of Afro-American youth participating in legend trips, so the activity may be a cultural inheritance of people from Europe. The percentage of teenagers who experience a legend trip at least once is unknown, because there is no national survey of this activity. However, several localized studies indicate that between 14 percent and 28 percent of teenagers have participated in a legend trip.[15] These activities have been going on for generations, long before the current Satanic cult scare.

The remnants of adolescent legend trips are commonly mistaken by police "experts" on ritualistic crime, local clergymen, and newspaper reporters, for indicators of teenage Satanism or Satanic cult activity. What is seen as an "altar" for a Satanic sacrifice, may really have been a makeshift altar or a campfire site for a legend trip. "Satanic" graffiti spray-painted on the walls inside an abandoned old house, or on trees in a secluded wooded area, may really be the ersatz magical inscriptions necessary for an exciting legend trip. Similarly, more serious remnants of juvenile delinquency, such as mutilated animals and vandalized cemeteries, are commonly products of legend trips.[16]

So-called occult-related crime is primarily a matter of petty juvenile crime.

When teenagers sometimes leave behind symbols widely regarded as being Satanic, they have a new and rather effective way of shocking adults, particularly adults in communities where many people believe that Satan is a being, prowling the world in search of souls. Some teenagers may now act out a parody of Satanic cult activity, in order to shock adults who read about their delinquent antics in the local newspaper and take it very seriously as evidence of dangerous Satanists in the area. Photographs in newspapers of graffiti symbols on overturned tombstones are easily seen by adults through the distorting lens of preconceptions about teenage Satanism.

Juvenile delinquents involved in pseudo-Satanism

In 1990, the Michigan State Police conducted a careful survey of "occult-related" crimes reported by law enforcement agencies in that state.[17] Only 22 percent of the responding agencies reported having investigated any "occult-related" crimes, much less than popular concern in rural areas and small towns might suggest. The vast majority of these crimes, 74 percent, involved graffiti, vandalism, the mutilation and killing of domestic or farm animals, and cemetery desecrations. (Only 1 percent involved homicides.) Almost all of the people who committed "occult-related" crimes were young, white males. Only 8 percent of the offenders were over the age of twenty-five and most were teenagers.

Inquiries about the offenders' training in occult matters revealed that in almost all cases the offenders were self-taught from sources that included friends, heavy metal rock music, movies, magazines, and books. In other words, so-called occult-related crime is primarily a matter of petty juvenile crime. Most importantly, the study concluded that the occult practices and paraphernalia in these kinds of crimes are a "red herring across the trail, distracting the investigator from real issues or motives in the case."[18]

Many "occult-related" juvenile crimes are products of adolescent legend trips. However, additional circumstances also account for "occult-related" juvenile delinquency. We can get a better understanding of what is happening, if we carefully examine the reliable research about pseudo-Satanist juvenile delinquents in the broader context of what we know about teenage crime in general.

In behavioral science, attempts to understand aggressive criminal behavior have led to the identification of two basic kinds of factors which contribute to such behavior: 1) personality dispositions toward deviant (meaning rule-breaking) aggressive behavior; and 2) group influences upon the person from participation in deviant subcultures which promote criminal behavior.

The beliefs and values which a person uses to justify (to excuse) their aggressive and criminal behavior is usually learned and strengthened in a deviant group subculture. Criminologists refer to these beliefs and values as a "deviant ideology." A deviant ideology functions to neutralize possible feelings of guilt. No particular beliefs are intrinsically deviant. Satanic beliefs can be used as a deviant ideology to justify aggression. So can beliefs about masculine ("Macho") pride. Even beliefs about God, Christ, or the Bible can be used as a deviant ideology by some people to justify their aggressive acts.

When people justify murder in terms of their personal Christian beliefs, we don't attribute the cause to the Christian religion. Instead, we seek the causes of their aggression in their particular personality dispositions and group influences. We must do the same when we learn about some vicious act of aggression committed by a teenager, who justifies what he or she has done by referring to some self-taught Satanist beliefs. It is misleading to focus too much attention on the excuse of Satanist beliefs, no matter how repulsive we may find them.

The ritual acts and group beliefs of these delinquents does not constitute a religion anymore than do the ritual acts and group beliefs of teenage gang members, or than those of the Ku Klux Klan. Almost all teenagers who even profess to be Satanists lack any elaborate belief system focussed upon Devil worship. Instead, they have fabricated a deviant ideology in order to: justify their underlying personality dispositions to express aggressive hostility; or justify rebellion from adult social restrictions; or obtain public notoriety. This is what I mean when I refer to teenagers as "pseudo-Satanist" delinquents rather than as "teenage Satanists."

Research findings about pseudo-Satanist delinquents

There are very few genuinely scientific studies of teenage pseudo-Satanists. At this point, the most careful study of these juvenile delinquents has been done by Kelly Richard Damphousse, in 1991.[19] Damphousse studied 55 juvenile delinquents involved in some degree of "Devil worship," and compared them with 475 juvenile delinquents who were not involved in such activity. All of the teenagers were incarcerated at the Texas Youth Commission Reception Center, in Brownwood, Texas. All of them were interviewed using a sixty-one-page questionnaire about their drug use, delinquent behavior, school activities, family and peer relationships, and personality, as well as their involvement in Satanism. Damphousse identified the teenagers who were involved in "Satanism," by means of their own admission that they had taken part, at least once, in some kind of "formal ceremony to worship Satan or the devil."[20] The information was then carefully analyzed, using statistical techniques to compare the two samples of juvenile delinquents.

Almost all teenagers who even profess to be Satanists lack any elaborate belief system focussed upon Devil worship.

The pseudo-Satanist juvenile delinquents differed from the other juvenile delinquents in several ways. 1) They were more likely to be white, rather than Afro-American. 2) They were more likely to be from middle class backgrounds, rather than working class or poor backgrounds. 3) They were more likely to have high intelligence scores on an I.Q. test, rather than average scores. 4) They were more likely to heavily use hallucinogenic drugs, rather than other kinds of drugs, such as cocaine or heroin, or no drugs. 5) They were more likely to feel that they had little power or control over their lives, rather than see themselves as having some degree of control over lives. 6) Finally, they were just as likely to be females as males, rather than mostly males. In other ways, the two sets of juvenile delinquents were similar. The research also found that the delinquents who participated in Satanic ceremonies, did so as part of a group activity, indicating that they were not social loners as is popularly believed.

In other words, white, middle class, highly intelligent teenagers, who have a high need for control in their lives, are those who are most likely to justify their criminal activity in terms of a Satanist deviant ideology. It is important to keep in mind that these findings apply only to imprisoned pseudo-Satanist delinquents. So, we can't be sure how widely they can be applied to pseudo-Satanist delinquents who have not been arrested and imprisoned.

Damphousse also sought to determine whether this pseudo-Satanist juvenile delinquency develops through some special circumstances. He could not find any truly unique circumstances. In terms of family relationships, peer group attachment, alienation from school, and personal problems, the pseudo-Satanist delinquents had backgrounds similar to those of other delinquents. Therefore, Damphousse concluded that teenagers become involved in pseudo-Satanist delinquency through essentially the same circumstances as other juvenile delinquents.[21]

A psychological analysis of pseudo-Satanist delinquency

If we expect to be able to deal effectively with teenagers who commit crimes attributed to pseudo-Satanism, we must first have an accurate appraisal of the underlying psychological causes of such criminal behavior. Explaining such behavior as being a product of religious "cult" brainwashing and the influence of evil religious beliefs is dramatic, but entirely misleading. The behavior of teenagers engaged in pseudo-Satanism needs to be understood in the context of what we know about juvenile delinquency.

There is no single, comprehensive explanation of juvenile delinquency, nor can there ever be one. The criminal behavior in this catch-all category includes everything from truancy to murder. Therefore, we need to focus upon understanding specific forms of criminal behavior. Almost all of the crimes attributed to teenage pseudo-Satanists involve vandalism of cemeteries, churches and abandoned old houses, and the mutilation and killing of animals. Therefore, we need to ask about what satisfactions are obtained by young people through these kinds of behaviors. Simply calling the behavior "irrational" is meaningless circular logic and gets nowhere toward any understanding.

Explaining [criminal] behavior as being a product of religious "cult" brainwashing and the influence of evil religious beliefs is dramatic, but entirely misleading.

Some psychological insight into teenage pseudo-Satanist delinquency can be gleaned from a study of a small number of emotionally disturbed teens who were patients in a psychiatric clinic affiliated with a university in Canada.[22] The study collected information from therapy sessions given to eight adolescents, ages thirteen to sixteen, who were in treatment for a variety of anxiety-related disorders and aggressive behaviors. It is not surprising, considering that they were admitted for psychotherapy, that most of them came from disrupted, dysfunctional families, or that most were involved in aggressive crimes against property. Six of the eight were heavy users of hallucinogenic drugs before they developed any interest in Satanism, and none of them were involved in any kind of Satanic religious organization. The "Satanism" of these youths consisted of making Satanic drawings and listening to heavy metal rock music (all eight), to participation in makeshift "Black Masses" (seven), to the sacrifice of small animals (two).

Another series of case studies offers several sensitive portraits of emotionally disturbed teenagers who used magic ritualism to deal with their psychological problems. One case is that of a sixteen-year-old, who was undergoing psychotherapy for recurrent depression, severe identity problems (borderline personality disorder), and the abuse of hallucinogenic drugs.[23] The youth first became involved with Satanic ritualism, at the age of eleven, after attending a "Satanic mass" with some friends. The most common ritual that he engaged in was one of his own creation, which he called making proposals. In this ritual, he concentrated his thoughts on making a request to the Devil to harm someone through his use of mental telepathy. The teenager developed elaborate beliefs around this supposedly magical ritual, involving calling up spirits and demons. The therapist suggested that the boy relied upon this magical thinking and ritualism in order to obtain feelings of power and control in his life.

When the claims-makers focus our attention upon so-called Satanic beliefs, symbols, and rituals, they deflect our attention away from the real underlying problems of teenagers involved in pseudo-Satanism. It is much more useful to find out why so many emotionally disturbed and delinquent teenagers suffer from severe feelings of powerlessness and feelings of hostility. That should be the focus of our concern.

The rewards of vandalism and black magic

A very useful understanding of the satisfactions gained from vandalism can be found in the book *The Seductions of Crime,* by Jack Katz, a sociologist specialized in research on deviant behavior.[24] Katz used self-reported biographical descriptions from people who committed crimes, in an effort to determine the meaning the criminal behavior has to the people who actually engaged in that behavior (in contrast to taking for granted the meanings that are attributed to the crimes by victims or law enforcement officials). Katz's exposition of the satisfactions of vandalism demonstrates that the goals are symbolic and emotional, and largely function to enhance the vandal's feelings of power in being able to engage in such deviant behavior (rule-breaking).

The vandal doesn't obtain any material benefit from the behavior, and the evidence of the crime is always deliberately left behind. The main satisfaction found in vandalism by those who engage in it is the excitement of playing a kind of game, in which the challenge is to "get away with something" forbidden. When the vandal "gets away with it," he can feel a sense of accomplishing something which requires risk. Because the vandal subjectively defines his behavior in this way, it can also provide a feeling of self-affirmation, a sense of uniqueness and distinctiveness. (It is the feeling of "I am somebody.")

The practice of Satanic black magic rituals doesn't cause teenagers to engage in vandalism and animal mutilation.

Secondly, the behavior is an attack on the moral order of society and, thus, provides an outlet for feelings of hostility toward conventional society. Vandalism can be especially exciting if the objects of desecration are commonly defined as being sacred, as is the case with graves and churches. In such cases, the "forbiddenness" of the act of vandalism is heightened. Vandalism is the projection onto a public screen, of a negative, deliberately offensive identity, demanding attention. Finally, vandalism functions as an act which enhances group bonding, as adolescents share in a kind of secret, conspiratorial team effort.

The practice of Satanic black magic rituals doesn't cause teenagers to engage in vandalism and animal mutilation. Instead, such activity is drawn from the same package of subjective meanings. Makeshift black magic rituals offer the excitement of getting away with socially tabooed, deviant behavior, assaulting the moral order of conventional society, and bonding adolescents together in a secret, forbidden activity. The black magic rituals provide teenagers, who suffer from severe feelings of powerlessness, with an ersatz sense of empowerment. Their feelings of empowerment are heightened when teenagers take the magic rituals seriously, as if the rituals actually provide them with some kind of power to shape their social environment. If disapproving adults also take the magic rituals seriously, in either fear or anger, rather than ridicule them, those adults inadvertently reinforce the teenagers' attraction to black magic.

The development of a deviant identity

If we are really to understand these adolescents, we must first comprehend how someone can find emotional satisfaction in strongly condemned deviant behavior. How can a person feel *good* about being *bad?* How can a deliberately offensive identity be satisfying to some teenagers, or even adults for that matter?

Another research study of teenagers involved in vandalism offers some insight into how adolescents can develop a self-concept centered upon the satisfactions of deviant behavior.

> Once the boys acquired an image of themselves as deviants, they selected new friends who affirmed that self-image. As that self-conception became more firmly entrenched, they also became willing to try new and more extreme deviances. With their growing alienation came freer expression of disrespect and hostility for the representatives of the legitimate society. The disrespect increased the community's negativism, perpetuating the entire process of commitment to deviance.[25]

Sociologists call this gradual process, the development of a *deviant identity.* Deviant identities emerge out of the meanings people attribute to their own behavior, which in turn, may bear the mark of other people's reactions to deviant behavior. Deviant identities are, in a basic sense, chosen by the people themselves and are not simply the by-products of the detrimental influences of other people. Nevertheless, the condemnation of other people weighs heavily on the development of anyone's self-perception.

The process of acquiring a deviant identity can begin at a very early age, long before adolescents become involved in any serious criminal activity. A child's self-concept of being a "bad kid" emerges gradually, as a result of experiencing constant humiliations, insults, and rejection at the hands of others. There is abundant research evidence showing that aggressive teenage delinquents experience more frequent humiliations to their self-esteem during childhood than do non-delinquents, from parents, peers, and school teachers.[26] The feelings of being shamed are projected outward in constant hostility and anger.

Children with the self-image of being a bad kid experience the pain of feeling shame in their own eyes, to be sure. However, such self-images also offer certain potential emotional satisfactions.[27] This helps to account for their tenacity. Bad kids get a lot of attention, which is preferable to being ignored. Bad kids attract a circle of friends with similar self-concepts, which is preferable to being socially isolated. Bad kids also often have the power to scare "good kids" simply by their reputations. (There should be no illusions here; many "bad kids" are downright nasty, malicious, and even sadistic.) Ultimately, choosing the self image of being a bad kid is preferable to having an ambiguous, ill-defined identity.

An evil self-concept

In a few children, the self-concept of being a bad kid can go to an extreme, such as when children regard themselves as being "evil" people. This is most likely to happen when children have authoritarian, punitive parents, who use religious threats to humiliate and control them.[28] Michael Beck, a psychotherapist, has written about his own inner experience of having an "evil" self-concept as a child.

> I lived in constant dread of committing a mortal sin and dying without being forgiven. . . . Imagine yourself as being in some precarious position . . . and not knowing quite how you got there. Unrelieved dread leaves its indelible impression, and since anxiety generalizes, one grows apprehensive that things not evil are indeed evil merely because one becomes anxious about them.
>
> This is a particularly taxing issue during adolescence, when one is constantly preoccupied with sex. It is a mortal sin to think about sex. The prescription for handling sexual impulses is suppression. Since, whatever is suppressed intensifies and seeks expression, one is forced to handle a sticky wicket—so to speak.[29]

Beck goes on to explain how some people who develop an "evil" self-image can lead themselves to believe that their behavior is being controlled by the Devil.

> With even more damaged patients who think they are evil, the issue of their ability to deal with anger becomes a priority. They often turn anger against themselves. The extreme is the patient who becomes totally or partially identified with evil and feels that she or he is either Jesus Christ or the devil, or possibly believes the devil is controlling him or her.[30]

These observations by Beck that some people have a self-concept of being "evil" provide insight into why some teenage delinquents may be drawn to Satanic beliefs, in order to justify their aggressive behavior. Adolescents who see themselves as being "evil," create a psychological environment consistent with their self-concept. They see the world as they see themselves, a place where malicious evil is more genuine than compassion.

A therapist's description of a seventeen-year-old girl involved in pseudo-Satanism illustrates the point.

> Christina was also using satanism to rebel against her parents' religion. She did not keep her satanism a secret from her family. When her mother asked her directly about her satanic beliefs, Christina told her mother that there was nothing good in the world and that was why she liked satanism.[31]

It is quite likely that a great many pseudo-Satanist teenagers are rebelling from an overly restrictive, traditional religious family background which emphasizes that the world is an evil place. The possibility needs to be investigated.

Social influences upon teenage pseudo-Satanism

Many of the claims-makers assert that average adolescents can suddenly be transformed into hostile, aggressive delinquents, simply by their becoming involved in Satanic ritualism. This kind of claim appears to suggest that some kind of religious conversion process is at work, very similar perhaps to the process of becoming a "born-again" Christian and giving up one's past sinful ways, only with a reverse conversion from virtue to sinfulness. The claim has dramatic appeal. However, it is entirely inconsistent with what we know about the development of juvenile delinquency.

Most of the claims-makers also insist on viewing teenage pseudo-Satanism as being primarily a form of religious behavior, albeit in pursuit of evil religious beliefs. This model of thinking about teenage pseudo-Satanism as a process of religious conversion logically leads to an emphasis upon Satanic beliefs and magic rituals as the cause of the aggressive and criminal behavior. So, it is not surprising that one hears an elaborate presentation of purported Satanic symbols, religious beliefs, and black magic rituals at public seminars about youth involved in Satanism, while one hears very little about the psychology and sociology of juvenile delinquency.[32]

It is quite likely that a great many pseudo-Satanist teenagers are rebelling from an overly restrictive, traditional religious family background.

Much is also made about the supposed influence of Anton LaVey's Church of Satan in drawing teenagers into Satanism, primarily through their reading of his book, *The Satanic Bible*.[33] Some of the claims-makers also assert that a secret conspiracy of adult Satanists are recruiting young people into Satanism, operating as secret cults across the country. Again, this assertion appears to be drawn from a religious model of thinking. The analogy applied here is one in which adult proselytizers recruit youth in psychological crisis to their religion. However, there is simply no evidence for this kind of speculation. The claims-makers are weaving a tapestry out of their own imaginations and fears.

The social dynamics of a self-fulfilling prophecy

What social influences can account for the increasing use of Satanic beliefs by some teenagers as a deviant ideology to justify aggressive and criminal behavior? One social process at work is that of the self-fulfilling prophecy. The more attention given to the dangers of "Satanism" among youth, the more curious aggression-prone teenagers become about it, and the more some of them dabble in makeshift black magic.

The social process is similar to that which led to the rapid increase in the "hippie" subculture during the mid-1960s. The small number of strange countercultural youth in Haight-Ashbury were given sensationalized attention in the mass media. It was a dramatic story. Then, as the mass media reports were imitated by young people in other cities, the numbers of would-be "hippies" grew rapidly. Once they were widely condemned in public presentations, they were imitated by even more rebellious youth. (Remember the billboards urging teenagers to "get a haircut"?)

This does not imply that the mass media created teenage pseudo-Satanism. It didn't. Certainly, much of the newspaper sensationalism contributed to its spread. Paradoxically, most of the attention was drawn to it by local police, social workers, and clergymen, in their public lectures condemning teenage Satanism. What this self-fulfilling prophecy means is that a society often gets the kinds of deviants it fears and condemns most.

The Satanic symbolism fad among teenagers

With all of the publicity condemning certain symbols as being Satanic, it was inevitable that many teenagers would adopt those same symbols as a way of "shocking" adult authorities. Using so-called Satanic symbolism has become a fad among many teenagers. This is neither new nor surprising. Adolescents have a way of finding exactly those things which will disturb adults the most. This is especially the case during the early teenage years when they are striving to exert their independence from adult authority. Many teenage rebels are now affixing these taboo symbols on their clothes, scribbling them on their school notebooks, drawing them on their arms, and spraying them on walls, along with other messages offensive to adult sensibilities. These decorative insults do not, of course, constitute any kind of Devil worship, but the fad can lead a few curious teenagers toward an interest in makeshift black magic.

Once a young person develops an interest in things "Satanic," he or she can learn a lot about the so-called arts of black magic by simply visiting the local library. It is easy for a teenager to put together a concoction of "Satanic beliefs" from newspaper articles, from popular folklore, from horror movies, and even from what is learned in church about the Devil. He or she doesn't need to read *The Satanic Bible*.

It is highly unlikely that teenage pseudo-Satanists have any contact with organized Satanic religious groups, and it is very far-fetched to claim that criminals are recruiting teenagers into a secret Satanic Mafia. Such claims are similar to those made in the 1960s by some public officials, that the Communists were responsible for organizing college student radicals. In reality, of course, most student radicals put together their bits and pieces of social philosophy mainly through conversations between themselves. Very few of them read any books by Marx or Lenin, which they regarded as being quite tedious. Similarly, it is unlikely that many of today's pseudo-Satanist teenagers read much complicated occult theology.

The rootlessness of many teenagers

It is a matter of speculation why so many teenagers today have feelings of powerlessness, but it may well be because so many teenagers today are rootless. I suspect that one of the circumstances which draws together bands of adolescents into pseudo-Satanic ritualism in search of power over their fate is their alienation from stable family and friendship groups. Rootlessness is commonplace among lower class adolescents who live in urban poverty. However, similar conditions are also being experienced by more and more middle class adolescents.

With all of the publicity condemning certain symbols as being Satanic, it was inevitable that many teenagers would adopt those same symbols as a way of "shocking" adult authorities.

The criminologist Gwynn Nettler suggests that advanced, industrial societies are producing more and more unwanted youth from fragmented families, youth who are disconnected from stabilizing adult influences.[34] Many of these youth account for the seemingly senseless crimes of aggression which plague modern community life.

Connectedness to caring intimates is one of the prerequisites for adequate self-esteem, for having a self-image as an appreciated, unique, and "good" person.[35] I believe that those middle class teenagers who are most likely to be drawn into pseudo-Satanism are those who are disconnected from loving and caring parents and/or are ostracized from conventional middle class peers at school. They are likely to experience themselves as inhabiting a hostile, uncaring world, in which people's maliciousness is more real than their love. For them, evil is more real than goodness.

What can be done to help teenagers?

Teenage pseudo-Satanism presents a problem for many parents and communities. Beyond understanding it, what can be done?

It is likely to be self-defeating to attract a lot of public attention to the supposed dangers of teenage pseudo-Satanism. When so-called experts in teenage Satanism are brought into communities to lecture at schools and churches, one unintended effect is that they provoke curiosity about Satanism among hostile, marginalized adolescents. Ironically, these "experts" even provide youthful rebels with the Satanic symbolism, rituals, and beliefs, which they use to fabricate new ways to shock adult authorities.

A report about claims concerning teenage Satanism designed for teachers and school administrators sums up the basic findings of this chapter and the kind of recommendations most useful for schools.

> ... it appears that Satanic beliefs, when coupled with deviancy is an outcome of something more basic. In most cases, both the Satanic beliefs and the deviancy are symptoms of more fundamental personal problems. A symptom is not a cause. Thus, personal problems, rather than Satanic beliefs, should be the target for school or community intervention.
>
> In fact, any school intervention which narrowly defines its purpose as an effort to purge Satanic beliefs from the stu-

dent body is inappropriate. Such activity is more likely to make Satanism attractive. A far more prudent choice is for schools to build programs designed to help overcome personal problems such as substance abuse, academic failure, low self-esteem, child abuse, suicidal tendencies, or a pervasive sense of alienation. Inappropriate concerns over Satanic activity may serve to distract educators from developing programs which address serious problems known to affect many students.[36]

It would be useful for community agencies to develop youth programs aimed at enhancing the self-esteem of socially ostracized and alienated, middle class adolescents. The state of California is already developing such a program.[37] However, it is extremely difficult for social agencies to provide intimacy and genuine caring when these comforts are lacking from parents and peer groups.

Some teenagers who aspire to be Satanists are responding with rage to their own self-hatred. It is a self-hatred born out of lives empty of the love which heals. Perhaps the most malignant evil of our time is the harm caused by neglect and indifference, in societies offering abundant material satisfactions at the cost of poverty in human relatedness.

Notes

1. W.H. Auden, "September 1, 1939," *W.H. Auden, Selected Poems,* ed. Edward Mendelson, (New York: Random House, 1976).

2. Pat Pulling, *The Devil's Web* (Lafayette, LA: Huntington House, 1989), pp. 41–42.

3. Ronald M. Holmes, "Youth in the Occult: A Model of Satanic Involvement," *The Journal* (Official Publication of the National Fraternal Order of Police, vol. 18, no. 3 [Summer 1989]: 20–23; reprinted in *CJA File,* pp. 13–20, quote from p. 16–17).

4. Paula K. Lundberg-Love, "Update on Cults Part I: Satanic Cults," *Family Violence Bulletin* (Summer 1989): 9–10, published by University of Texas at Tyler.

5. Lundberg-Love, 1989, p. 9.

6. Bill Ellis, "Adolescent Legend-Tripping," *Psychology Today,* August 1983, 68–69; Bill Ellis, "Legend-Trips and Satanism: Adolescents' Ostensive Traditions as 'Cult' Activity," *The Satanism Scare,* ed. J. Richardson, J. Best, and D. Bromley (New York: Aldine de Gruyter, 1991), pp. 279–96.

7. Jan Harold Brunvand, *The Study of American Folklore: An Introduction,* 3rd edition (New York: W. W. Norton, 1986).

8. Ellis, 1983; Ellis, 1991.

9. Ellis, 1983, p. 68.

10. Ellis, 1991.

11. Ellis, 1983.

12. Ellis, 1991.

13. Ellis, 1983.

14. Ellis, 1991.

15. *Ibid.*

16. *Ibid.*
17. Michigan Department of State Police, "Michigan State Police Occult Survey," (Investigative Service Bureau, Michigan Department of State Police, June, 1990).
18. *Ibid.*, p. 9.
19. Kelly Richard Damphousse, *Did the Devil Make Them Do It? An Examination of the Etiology of Satanism among Juvenile Delinquents.* (Unpublished Masters Thesis, Department of Sociology, Texas A & M University, May 1991.)
20. Damphousse, 1991, p. 30.
21. Damphousse, 1991.
22. Dominique Bourget, Andre Gagnon, and John Bradford, M.W., "Satanism in a Psychiatric Adolescent Population," *Canadian Journal of Psychiatry* 33, no. 3 (April 1988): 197–202.
23. Amy M. Speltz, "Treating Adolescent Satanism in Art Therapy," *The Arts In Psychotherapy* 17 (Summer 1990): 147–55.
24. Jack Katz, *The Seductions of Crime*, (New York: Basic Books, 1988).
25. William J. Chambliss, "The Saints and the Roughnecks," *Society* 11, no. 1 (Nov./Dec. 1973); reprinted in *Deviance: The Interactionist Perspective*, 4th ed., ed. Earl Rubington and Martin S. Weinberg (New York: Macmillan, 1981), pp. 236–47, (p. 246).
26. Thomas J. Scheff, Suzanne M. Retzinger, and Michael T. Ryan, "Crime, Violence and Self-Esteem: Review and Proposals," *The Social Importance of Self-Esteem*, ed. Andrew M. Mecca, Neil Smelser, and John Vasconcellos, (Berkeley, CA: University of California, 1989), pp. 165–99.
27. Morris Rosenberg, Carmi Schooler, and Carrie Schoenbach, "Self-Esteem and Adolescent Problems: Modeling Reciprocal Effects," *American Sociological Review* 54, no. 6 (1989): 1004–1018.
28. C. Daniel Batson and W. Larry Ventis, *The Religious Experience: A Social-Psychological Perspective* (New York: Oxford University Press, 1982). (See chapter 7, "Mental Health or Sickness?")
29. Michael Beck, "Acquisition and Loss of an Evil Self-Image," *Evil: Self and Culture*, ed. Marie C. Nelson and Michael Eigen (New York: Human Sciences Press, 1984), pp. 170–80, (p. 172).
30. Beck, 1984, p. 177.
31. Speltz, 1990, p. 150.
32. Robert D. Hicks, *In Pursuit of Satan: The Police and the Occult* (Buffalo, N.Y.: Prometheus Press, 1991).
33. Anton S. LaVey, *The Satanic Bible* (New York: Avon, 1969).
34. Gwynn Nettler, *Killing One Another* (Cincinnati, Ohio: Anderson, 1982).
35. Aminah Clark, Harris Clemes, and Reynold Bean, *How to Raise Teenagers' Self-Esteem* (Los Angeles: Price, Stern and Sloan, 1978).
36. Jeff Brookings and Alan McEvoy, "Satanism and Schools," *School Intervention Report* 3, no. 5 (April–May 1990), Learning Publications Inc.: Holmes Beach, Florida, pp. 9–10.
37. California State Department of Education, *Toward A State of Esteem*, The Final Report of the California Task Force to Promote Self-Esteem and Personal and Social Responsibility, January, 1990; Andrew M. Mecca, Neil J. Smelser, and John Vasconcellos, eds., *The Social Importance of Self-Esteem* (Berkeley, CA: University of California, 1989).

7

Claims of Satanic Ritual Abuse Are Unsubstantiated

Sharma Oliver

Sharma Oliver is a registered therapist and freelance writer.

There are no cults that practice satanic ritual abuse (SRA). Despite accusations of SRA that number in the tens of thousands, not one case has been substantiated. The phenomenon of "recovered memory"—in which a person experiences horrible abuse over several years, then completely forgets about it but suddenly remembers it with the help of a therapist—is the result of fevered imaginations running amuck. The existence of satanic cults that practice ritual abuse is an urban myth fueled by societal fears of and fascination with sexuality.

There are NO satanic ritual child abuse cults. A pretty bold statement? How about this one: It is not possible to experience horrible abuse over the course of several years, such abuse including being forced to participate in rape, murder and cannibalism, completely forget about it and then, with the help of a therapist, support group or instruction book, suddenly remember it in shocking detail. Those who claim this scenario is possible ignore both scientific research and the fact that those "recovered" memories, while full of lurid sexual and other abuse, commonly neglect to include details that could prove that the events took place.

Current research on the brain, and memory, simply does not support the idea that a person could forget years of hideous experiences and remember them later. Some of these "recovered" memories have contained information that is possible to disprove, for example remembered abuse set in the attic of a house that does not have an attic. Many of the proponents of "recovered" memories refuse to address either side of this issue, instead accusing doubters of further abusing the "survivors" by not believing them.

As far as "satanic ritual abuse" by Devil-worshipping cults goes, a study funded by National Center on Child Abuse and Neglect (NCCAN), completed in the fall of 1994, asked 6,900 psychologists, psychiatrists and social workers, and 4,655 district attorneys, child protective services and police organizations, how many cases of the satanic ritual abuse they had ever found. While they reported over 12,000 accusations, not one actual, proven instance that even slightly approached the stories reported by "survivors" turned up.

There have been a few cases of individual criminals who claimed their crimes were satanically inspired as part of an argument that they were not responsible for their crimes, a few instances of gangs of drug dealers led by individuals who used what they claimed were satanic rituals to control the gang and supposedly protect it, one case of a married couple who practiced what might be considered magickal/sexual rites involving themselves and their underage son and quite a few incidents of vandalism and minor crimes committed by small groups of teenagers who were doing the usual teenage rebellious stuff. In each case the media whipped the public into a frenzy with stories of satanic activity. When the stories later fell apart, little attention was paid by those in search of an audience.

The study found NO evidence of any sort of the organized ritual abuse networks, intergenerational groups or international groups reported by "survivors."

A similar study in Great Britain of 84 cases of child sexual abuse spanning three years that involved accusations of satanic abuse also found zero evidence of the existence of any sort of satanic activity.

Kenneth Lanning, FBI agent in Quantico, Virginia has become the top ritualistic abuse investigator in the country. He has repeatedly stated that there are NO satanic ritual child abuse cults in existence in this country, let alone multigenerational and multinational ones.

The existence of satanic child abuse cults, like the "alligators in the sewers," "Kentucky fried rats," "Snuff Porn," and "Poisoned Halloween Candy," is an urban myth. These stories are widely believed to be true but are not. Such stories may serve to externalize societal fears and give people something to guard against. Better a known danger, even if false, than just living with the relentless stress of change which leaves one feeling helpless to act. To date, there is absolutely no evidence for satanic ritual child abuse cults. However, it is impossible to prove that something that did not happen, did not happen.

Many books, articles and studies have been published discussing this hysteria, and many websites exist which deal with both false accusations of child abuse and the aftermath for those accused and the children coerced into making these accusations. Further sources of information are listed at the end of this article.

Repressed and recovered memories— how did this happen?

I will mainly address satanic ritual child abuse and the current sexual and moral panic in our society in this article, but keep in mind that this satanic ritual abuse panic, and the thousands of accusations against families, daycare centers, schools, churches and neighbors, could not be happening without a belief in both "repressed" or "recovered" memories and in the widespread occurrence of child sexual abuse.

While most mainstream professional therapy organizations are now more cautious about "recovered" memories, many still refuse to criticize their members who practice it or take meaningful steps to prevent client abuse via this methology. Over the last twenty years this hysteria has swept through law enforcement, nursing, social work, therapy, and the various body therapies. Too many members of these professions are still "believers." The therapeutic professions and the professionals who work in child abuse prevention have been a growth industy for the last few decades; it is in their financial interest to foster the idea that there is an epidemic of child abuse, both satanic and sexual, taking place today.

Repressed and recovered memories simply do not exist in the form suggested by the widely published first person stories about it. While it is possible to forget individual childhood or adult events, even very traumatic ones, it is not possible to forget years of rape, beatings, cannablism, and murder.

There are also many instances of individuals in the past not labeling experiences that happened to them, or things that they did, as abuse that now would be considered such. When history and traditional power structures are reassessed, those experiences are sometimes seen in a different light. Slavery was not seen as wrong for much of human history and was supported by governments and religions. Beliefs change, for example much of what is now considered date rape was simply how sex often happened in my teen years (the 1950s) and some of what was then considered ordinary discipline would now be considered child abuse.

As a nation, we are obsessed with sex.

I have no intention of minimizing the damage done by rape and assault, trivializing excess punishment of children, excusing parents who treat their children badly or negating the distress many of us carry from our childhoods. At the same time, I invite everyone to consider their own memories. Don't you have quite clear memories of the traumatic events in your early years? Don't you recall all too clearly some experiences you only wish you could repress or forget? Twenty years of research done by Dr. Elizabeth Loftus at the University of Washington show that memory is quite malleable and that repressed memories of the type described, that is, years of unspeakable horror and abuse, do not exist.

What I find the most interesting about the subject of satanic child abuse is that so many people's minds are already made up, often without having done even the slightest amount of research, or after having studied only one point of view or listening to one story. It is not difficult to find material on this subject. Numerous books have been written from every possible point of view, and national newspaper, medical, legal, social science and other databases are available.

One thing all those sources say, even those who most fervently believe in satanic child abuse, is that there is no "hard" corroborating evidence. No locations, no bones, no bloodstains, no tunnels under McMartin Preschool, nothing to back up the improbable stories. All that exists are verbal reports from the alleged survivors, none of which have been verified by physical evidence, and some of which have been proven factually wrong.

Commonly those "memories" appear after the "survivor" has been hypnotized, participated in a survivors' support group or read a survivors' self-help book such as *The Courage to Heal* or *The Right To Innocence*. The previous, by Beverly Engel, advises in the introduction, "If you have ever had reason to suspect you may have been abused, even if you have no explicit memory of it, the chances are very high that you were." Really? Is there any other aspect of life to which this standard of reasoning applies?

It is a good idea to read books and articles from several points of view before deciding what you believe. And that includes this article.

The history of satanic and sexual panics

Guess who said each of the two quotes below, and what group they each referred to:

No. 1: "This cult is worthy of the customs from which it sprang. As for the initiation of new members, the details are as disgusting as they are well known. The novice himself, deceived by the coating of dough (covering a sacrificial infant), thinks the stabs are harmless. Then—it's horrible!—they hungrily drink the blood and compete with one another as they divide his limbs. And the fact they all share knowledge of the crime pledges them all to silence. On the feast-day they foregather with all their children, sisters, mothers, people of either sex and all ages. Now, in the dark, so favorable to shameless behavior, they twine the bonds of unnamable passion, as chance decides. Precisely the secrecy of this evil religion proves that all these things, or practically all, are true."

No. 2: "There is evidence that the cults perform human sacrifices, burying of children underground in animal carcasses, sexual acts with children, drinking of human blood, eating human flesh and torturing animals and humans."

Perhaps these are obvious because of the language used. However, it may come as a surprise to some readers that No. 1 is from Roman writer Minicus Felix in the first century A.D. He was referring to the upstart Christian cults that were seen as a threat to traditional Roman values. Quote No. 2 is from Jacquie Balodis, an expert in alleged satanic brainwashing techniques, printed in *The Edge of Evil: The Rise of Satanism in North America*, by Jerry Johnson.

In both instances, and in a multitude of other examples that fall between the two in time, the societies involved were under tremendous pressure. One way of life, one set of beliefs, was metamorphosing into what came next. Change equals stress for human beings, and even desirable changes require a period of disequilibrium before the new balance is reached. So change is seldom welcomed.

Whenever the social changes taking place look like they might drastically shift power from one person or group to others, or when the amount of change becomes so great as to be frightening, those who stand to lose, and those who fear change, fight against it with all their resources. We human beings want scapegoats to blame for our fear and anger. That is what is happening now. One means of doing so is to create an enemy, however spurious—satanic cult ritual child abusers—and fight it.

The dangers of childhood—abuse and power

The vast majority of child abuse, sexual or other, takes place within the child's immediate circle of family, caregivers and acquaintances. Over fifty percent of child abuse is neglect. Sexual abuse is the least common, accounting for 11–13 percent. Yet neglect, by far the largest problem, is often overlooked in favor of the much more exciting chance to go after those accused of child sexual abuse.

Most of this abuse, sexual and other, is done by one individual, with a small minority of it being done by two adults, usually a couple. Most child sexual abuse is seduction rather than rape or other violence. Sometimes lost in this discussion is that child abuse is wrong, whether done by individuals or by those in positions of authority in the guise of protecting children. Children needs adults to actually protect them.

In my opinion, the current hysteria over sexual abuse rings in daycare centers and Bible study groups is almost all the product of the fevered fantasies of the accusers and/or prosecutors running amuck expressed through four main groups. Those groups are religious extremists, the therapy establishment, the media, and fundamentalist feminism.

The hysteria is fueled by a wide range of behaviors and crimes lumped together under one umbrella, so the photos taken by grandparents of their grandchildren playing naked running through the sprinkler, or photos taken by parents of their children playing naked at a nudist camp, is "child pornography" just as surely as photos of children having sex with adults.

This happens in other areas of public concern and the collapsing of these categories, done to make them seem like a bigger social problem, confuses nearly everyone. For example, in one report on violence in the schools, a child making an aggressive motion with a pencil, a child bringing blunt paper scissors to school, a boy with an inch long plastic gun from a cereal box, and children with guns were all collapsed together under the warning that "over half of our children are coming to school armed."

The claims that surveys show that somewhere between one quarter and three quarters of women are sexually assaulted before age 18 neglect to mention that, in some surveys, seeing a flasher or receiving an obscene phone call is counted as an assault, along with rape. When categories are collapsed like this, it becomes difficult or impossible to assess if there is a problem which needs to be addressed and how to adddress it. And it fuels the public fear that society is spinning out of control.

It is interesting to note that the satanic abuse accusations happen almost exclusively within Caucasian groups.

In all of the big daycare child sexual abuse cases it was said that the children were being used to produce "child pornography." In zero of these cases was any such material introduced into evidence. While this certainly does not prove that none exists, it is interesting to note how quickly that charge is made and how it adds to the hysteria.

Why do the accusers do it? Some just want to make a name for themselves as being "tough on crime"; others are therapists or bureaucrats whose job it is to find evidence of child abuse and who get paid or funded in relation to how many victims they find.

The vast majority of these people appear to really believe in what they are doing. They are usually acting from laudable impulses, trying to protect children, but they have gone overboard. Parents fear for their children's safety and are frightened by these terrible stories, often not knowing what to believe. The results are often lucrative for those specializing in this field. While these people undoubtedly believe they're helping children, are they?

In 1974, in response to real needs, Walter Mondale proposed and saw passed into law the Child Abuse Prevention and Treatment Act, CAPTA. This legislation, which has been amended and made more draconian over the years, provided millions of dollars to state governments to set up child protection units, usually under the social services bureaucracy in each state. These millions came with a set of rules which have done at least as much harm as good. In order to get the money, states had to pass legislation which stated that no person making an accusation of child abuse in good faith could be held responsible for anything which happened to the accused or the child as a result. This was meant to protect those who would be afraid to make reports unless they had both anonymity and immunity from lawsuits.

In practice this meant that the police, prosecutors, social workers, neighbors, angry spouses during divorce proceedings, anyone . . . could make an accusation which would be thoroughly investigated no matter how improbable the charges. Plus the criteria for child abuse, particularly sexual abuse, has expanded to include normal parental touching if the state investigator decides it was improper.

Why do people believe these claims? All one has to do to see that these wild accusations cannot be true is to really examine what is being said. Go find and read the transcripts from the big daycare child abuse cases. Many of them are available on the internet or in books. In the McMartin case, the first to get wide publicity, children were hounded until they agreed that all manner of abuse had taken place. This including that a horse was killed with a baseball bat to frighten them. Stop and think. The average horse weighs between 800 and 1200 pounds. Not only would it be difficult to kill with a baseball bat, unless it was hit perfectly the first time it would probably thrash around, wreck the room, possible hurt some children. And what exactly could be done with the body?

Children in these cases have reported that they were taken up in spaceships, that they were raped with butcher knives, that snakes were put into their mouths, but for some reason they never mentioned any of this to their parents at the time because they were too scared. Of course no evidence of any of this other than the extremely doubtful testimony of children was ever introduced. There was never any medical evidence introduced showing the damage some of these actions would have caused, if they had actually happened. Children less than six years old were questioned repeatedly until they began making up stories to satisfy their interrogators.

But the accusers learned something important at McMartin. The children were videotaped in that case during their interrogations and those tapes showed to what lengths the questioners went to get the children to agree they had been abused. In fact, the accusers would not accept any answer other than the one they wanted. Jurors reported that seeing those tapes caused them to doubt the accusations. After that accusers avoided taping interviews saying that it was abusive to the children to be taped.

A few horrible and highly publicized cases of child abuse and murder further inflamed the public, and encouraged the government to pass yet more intrusive laws in the name of protecting children.

The facts as charged cannot stand examination, neither do the numbers hold up. In the case of satanic abuse, claims are made that between 50,000 and two million children are being sacrificed in satanic rites each year. If that were true, most of us would have lost a blood relative or at least know a family who has lost a child.

It is estimated that actually 300,000 children are reported missing each year. (Their pictures are on milk cartons.) So what happens to these children? Around 200,000 are taken by non-custodial parents in divorce fights, 100,000 run away or are thrown out by their parents and approximately 200 per year are kidnapped by strangers. While even one child being kidnapped and murdered is one too many, it does not require the existence of a vast, secret, international conspiracy of satanic cults to explain how these children disappear.

A report disseminated by the National Center on Child Abuse and Neglect (NCCAN) Child Maltreatment 1995, *Reports From the States to the National Child Abuse and Neglect Data System,* depicted more than three million reports of alleged child abuse and neglect that year. However, two million of those complaints were determined to be without foundation or false upon investigation. The ordeal these families were put through is dismissed as irrelevant by those who continue to imagine child abuse under every rock, and in every home.

The "crimina excepta" of our time

In Salem, Massachusetts in 1692, dozens of people were accused of practicing witchcraft based on "spectral" evidence. "Spectral" evidence is the signs of hysteria in accusers and reports from dreams and visions. Ordinary law had to be suspended to allow this evidence in. In Salem, the only ones executed were those who continued to deny their guilt. All who admitted it were fined or otherwise lightly punished and then released—except for the two dogs who were executed. It was impossible to discern how they pled, but they were convicted via "spectral" evidence, as were all the others. *The Devil in Massachusetts,* by Marion Starkey, details the execution of the 19 women and one man during that wave of satanic panic. As soon as the court ceased to accept spectral evidence, the trials ended.

Then, and during the Inquisition, normal rules of evidence and proof were ignored or superseded. People were tortured until they confessed to crimes that never occurred. This practice was named "crimina excepta" and was used for crimes considered so horrendous, and so dangerous to society, that all restraints upon legal procedures should be suspended. The crimes in that category during the Inquisition were heresy, treason and witchcraft. Now the "crimina excepta" in our society are sexual crimes with children and the sale of illegal drugs.

Social change and the urban myths of our times

There is no question that children are physically, emotionally and sexually abused in our society. Many more are also neglected. About 2,100 children per year are killed by their parents or caregivers. Given that so many horrible things are actually happening to children, what might cause people to believe that satanic or occult ritual child abuse cults exist or that ordinary people could forget years of vicious abuse and then remember it? Why is sexual abuse considered worse than neglect, beatings and even murder?

In my opinion, it is because the forces of change are so scary, and so impersonal, that they must be personified as something and someone. In a society such as ours, which both adores and fears sexuality, which uses sex to sell everything but tries to deny that it is doing so and which is going through so much major social change, the stress is overwhelming. We are fascinated by sex and want and need sexual information, but we don't approve of our own wants and needs.

Many people fantasize about the "good old days," before the Pill, when there was not so much teenage and other sex. But there were no such good old days. There may not have been as much sex, although I doubt it. I and all my close girlfriends got pregnant before we were married in the 1950s and early 1960s. About half of us got married; the other half slunk away in shame to not very secretly have babies and give them up for adoption. It's easier to think those "old days" were great if you were not there.

Our culture is saturated in sexual imagery. There are several layers or types of media presentation of sexuality in the United States, of varying levels of respectability. These layers include: sex education material; scientific and research material; sexually explicit media; informational material abut sexual minorities, (lesbian, gay, bisexual, transvestite and sadomasochistic (SM) literature and so on); the major "men's" and "women's" magazines; romance novels, (which make up the single largest genre in the fiction market and often feature stories of forced or semi-forced sex set in an exotic locale); movies; television entertainment, music, plays and other "cultural" media, which commonly have sexual themes; true crime magazines; tabloid newspapers; and lastly the mainstream newspapers, news magazines and television news presentations.

While the frankly sexually explicit, often referred to as pornography, seldom contain violence coupled with sex, sexualized violence is the main focus in much of mainstream entertainment. "Respectable" or mainstream news media seldom contain openly sexual information; instead, they sexually titillate us by reporting on the bizarre, the criminal and the scandalous.

Since even viewing "child pornography" on the internet, possessing it in your home and so on, are such serious crimes, we the public don't even know the nature of the media which is being used to whip us all into a frenzy. As ordinary heterosexual pornography became more available, and as the attacks against it mounted, more people sought it out, looked at it, and decided it was not a big deal. The same process is at work with gay erotica and even sadomasochistic erotica. But this will never happen with kiddie porn because only law enforcement and the special guardians of the public morals will ever see it.

Given the content and ratings of all these media, it's clear we want sexual information. But we won't tolerate what we consider to be child pornography: It is outside the protection of the First Amendment. However, if a story involving children and sex is presented as factual or as part of mainstream entertainment, particularly if it is violent, it is permissible and can be read or viewed even by people who would never allow themselves to look at ordinary sexually explicit media, let alone that featuring children. A mainstream movie such as *The Prince of Tides,* starring Nick Nolte and Barbra Streisand, can contain the brutal anal rape of a nine-year-old boy as its key scene without it being even mentioned in the reviews. After all, they killed the guys who did it and it was presented as awful, so it could not possibly be illegal, could it?

As a nation, we are obsessed with sex. Unfortunately we also fear it, and repress our own interest in it, so it must be disguised and made unpleasant or violent to quiet our fears that watching it might arouse us, and to make information about it something a respectable person needs to know. I feel that this "erotophobia," fear of erotic pleasure, is beneath at least some of the impulse behind both writing and reading the "satanic abuse" stories, and their popularity.

Just as this type of story in mainstream media has allowed and encouraged respectable people to read about and discuss sex, so the intensity of the attacks against pornography, "the gay-lesbian menace," sex education and "child sexual abuse" has created an audience for that media.

The strongest force behind the satanic ritual child abuse panic is people who fear, distrust and want to get rid of any religion other than their own version of conservative Christianity.

As an unintended result, members of the general public are becoming a great deal more knowledgeable about their own interests and desires, the gay and lesbian communities are becoming more and more known and accepted, more people have seen and will tolerate pornography, and bisexuality, a label generally unknown just a few years ago, is becoming an accepted sexual identification.

In my analysis, this American obsession, and fear, regarding sex illustrates our inner conflicts between our intellect and our deeper drives, fears, hopes and dreams. These conflicts are written out in the popular literature, particularly the urban myths, of the times. We project our fears, and our desires, onto some "other" who is not like us; our urban myths tell us who the current other is. Right now, our other is satanic, homosexual, criminal or alien—note that UFO abduction stories usually include sexual examinations.

When something is labeled as forbidden and dangerous, it is easy to wonder if it could possibly be all that bad. After all, the people telling us how bad the stuff is must have looked at it, and they seem more or less ok. Furthermore, the urge to take at least a peek is very strong, particularly if one is raised in a belief system that labels any sexual impulse as very dangerous. So not only does the reading of satanic child pornography, along with other types of sexual media, become permissible, it becomes almost an obligation to gain information to protect children and society. I believe that a similar shocked, yet titillated, voyeurism fuels the current pop fascination with sadomasochistic imagery.

Social/urban myths of the past

A type of urban myth began appearing about 1909 in the form of books and pamphlets decrying white slavery. These contained allegedly true stories of innocent young blond women, barely pubescent, being lured and forced into a life of degrading prostitution by a huge, secret and powerful conspiracy. This myth appeared at a time when thousands of young women were leaving the farms and small towns to go to work in big cities and prostitution was the "social vice." Then, as now, there were complex and difficult social changes taking place, and many yearned for a return to simpler times.

This literature, which many accused of containing not an iota of truth, served several purposes. It warned of the dangers of the big city. It mourned the loss of most of a generation of farm children to life in the cities. It described how a young woman could move to the city safely, the places and companions she should avoid and the pitfalls of leaving home. It allowed everyone to have a peek into the sordid life of prostitution and the red light districts, giving extremely graphic accounts of what took place there, without readers ever having to risk going to such places. And it blamed these evils all on dark and unsavory foreigners.

A previous iteration of this genre was the "white woman captured by the Indians" stories that circulated during early colonial times, in the 17th and 18th centuries.

And while not always specifically sexual, do not forget the McCarthy Communist witch hunts of the Fifties, the hundreds of years of persecution of the Jews or the multitudes of genocides around the world and throughout history in the name of mythical racial, religious or ideological purity. Usually those being attacked were accused of some sort of sexual perversion, if not several kinds.

The interval between these panics and waves of persecution is part of the key to their cyclic nature. Each one builds as fewer people who experienced the last one are alive to warn against repeating this type of social folly. Except for those who have made a particular study of McCarthy and J. Edgar Hoover, only people over age 60 would have much memory of how terrible the Communist purges were. If you go to the library and read about the hearings, it will remind you quite a lot of the flavor of our current panic.

Many of these types of stories also are a projection of the racial and ethnic fears of their intended audience. The stories usually show the "evil, sexual and dangerous" ones to be darker skinned, more savage, less civilized and more highly sexed. That theme is played out to this day, even in Disney films like the *Little Mermaid* with the evil seductress being darker, bustier and obviously sexier than the sweet, innocent, and ultimately triumphant redheaded princess. I wonder if the evil ones are blond or redhaired in darker-skinned societies?

It is interesting to note that the satanic abuse accusations happen almost exclusively within Caucasion groups. I know of no daycare or church child sexual abuse scandals among any other ethnic group. Are they less perverted than whites?

Social forces and current urban myths

I believe these current satanic ritual child abuse stories are part of a generalized panic our society is experiencing, pushed by an interesting combination of forces. The amount, and the pace, of change taking place now may be unprecedented. To get a perspective on what we are living through, you can read Marshall McLuhan, Alvin Toffler or a fairly new book, *The Saturated Self, Dilemmas of Identity in Modern Life*, by Kenneth J. Gergen.

In my opinion, the human species is attempting to coalesce into a world society, and we haven't a clue how to do it. Over 99 percent of our DNA is over 12 million years old. Until about 100 years ago, the average person never traveled over 25 miles from his or her place of birth and met only 200 other people, face to face, in his or her whole life. Now we can meet 200 people in one day, travel the world, and have to deal with a multicultural society that is fascinating but confusing.

For a long time, we could pull together as a nation because we had to outgun the Russians. Now we watch as their society disintegrates, and what enemy is left to organize against? If we do not have a real enemy, perhaps we have to make one up to satisfy the demands of a nervous system honed on over 12 million years of struggle.

And do not forget that the millennium is almost upon us. The folklore and urban legends about the significance of this particular flip of the calendar page are dire. When 999 was approaching 1000, much of Christianity freaked because they believed in the prophesies of that time, which also said the end of the world was near. When the world did not end in 1000, a backlash occurred, some groups became even more extreme and religious minorities were attacked anew. Now we have extremist branches of most religions. What panic will sweep the world as the calendar turns over?

The strongest force behind the satanic ritual child abuse panic is people who fear, distrust and want to get rid of any religion other than their own version of conservative Christianity. Added to this is a major industry that "educates" far right Christians, and any of the general public who get sucked in, regarding the dangers from Satanism, feminism, pornography, the homosexual menace, paganism, the New Age, meditation, sex education in schools, yoga, other world religions and the New World Order. The Christian far right and their allies are horrified that so many women are leaving the home to go to work, and that divorce is an option. What better way to convince them to stay home and stay married than to create a panic about daycare and other dangers to children? Most parents are uncertain about how much sexual information a child should have, and most would like the world to be safer.

The more extreme faction of this religious group sees the world in black and white terms and wants to return to an imagined earlier time when life was simpler, the roles of the sexes were distinct and separate and fewer people questioned the status quo. Any sexual information other than that which they provide their own children is objectionable to them.

Christian fundamentalists fight satanic hysteria

Not all Christians feel like this. Many responsible Christian groups are struggling with the issue of how to support members of their faith who make these bizarre satanic abuse claims, and who obviously need help of some kind, while not fueling the hysteria such claims create.

For example, *Satan's Underground: The Extraordinary Story of One Woman's Escape*, by Lauren Stratford, the pen name of Laurel Willson of Tacoma, Washington, was withdrawn by its publisher after Cornerstone, an evangelical Christian magazine published by Jesus People USA, exposed it as fraudulent. Unfortunately, another publisher re-issued it. And Ms. Willson continues to publish books about the "backlash" against "survivors" and speak on that subject at conferences where "recovered memory therapists" learn how to spot clients with "repressed memories" and help them remember.

Lauren's story raises an interesting question: Books which would be a felony to publish, sell, buy or perhaps even possess, because of their graphic content of children being raped and forced into nearly unspeakable sexual acts, are tolerated because they are said to be true. Should *Satan's Underground* now be considered child pornography, since it has been proven to be fiction, albeit poorly written fiction?

Cornerstone, in an effort to refocus Christians on real child abuse rather than side-tracking into sensationalism, also researched Mike Warnke, who wrote *The Satan Seller* and who lectures on the satanic circuit claiming to have been both a Satanist high priest and a member of the Illuminati before he was born again. Cornerstone exposed him as a fraud. For a wealth of information on how responsible religious people are working to expose the frauds in their midst and reduce social panic, visit the World Wide Web sites listed at this article's end. Keep in mind that these people have suffered satanic accusations themselves for exposing these liars who were preying on concerned and gullible Christians.

Other forces behind the panic

The next strongest social force behind the satanic ritual child abuse panic consists of therapists, police or former police officers and others who lecture, write books, consult, or lead workshops and training for therapists, police groups and concerned citizens, or who act as expert witnesses in trials and investigations. These leaders teach people to help identify, treat and counter the supposed threat from the forces of darkness. Therapists who have either had this training, or invented it on their own working one-on-one with clients, have convinced perhaps 50,000 clients that they have been satanically, ritually or otherwise sexually abused as children.

This segment of the problem would not exist without CAPTA and the millions of dollars poured into setting up a bureaucracy devoted to finding child abuse and combatting it. Crime Victims Compensation programs pay for the therapy of those who recover memories in many states. In Washington the state stopped this practice after a study showed that the longer people were in therapy for the treatment of repressed memories of childhood sexual abuse, the sicker they got.

Now, these were individuals who had no memory of childhood abuse before being exposed to the media or therapies that support these ideas. Nothing I am stating here should be taken to suggest that I do not believe that there are many survivors of childhood abuse with continuous memories. I know they exist and, in fact, fear that the current hysteria over spectral evidence will be used to distract society from dealing with the actual problems of abused children.

Another growth industry in therapy is in the discovery and treatment of people with multiple personalities, supposedly caused by satanic ritual or other sexual abuse in childhood. Before 1975 there were less than one hundred cases of multiple personality reported historically. *The Three Faces of Eve* was one of the earliest popular books on this subject. Now there are thousands of cases, a sub-specialty in therapy for the discovery and treatment of these patients, and dozens of books written by supposed survivors.

The third force driving this panic is a less-than-responsible mainstream news media.

Meanwhile, there is a significant growth industry in the area of satanic abuse self-publication, with desktop publishing pumping out titles like "I Was a Priest for Satan" and "How to Identify and Treat Survivors of Ritual Abuse Who Don't Know What's Wrong with Them" (I invented these titles, but they capture the flavor of the real ones). A huge bureaucracy has grown up at all levels of government around investigating families, identifying abused children and dealing with it. Billions of dollars has been, and continues to be, spent tearing families apart with false allegations of child sexual abuse. Satanic abuse allegations are not getting as much attention currently in the mainstream legal cases anymore, as those who pushed a belief in it are not winning in court very often. Many are being sued by those they hypnotized into believing their families tortured them.

The third force driving this panic is a less-than-responsible mainstream news media that puts accusations and suspicions of satanic crimes on Page 1, and when the facts come out a few days, weeks or months later, usually give them a two-inch mention on Page 27, if at all. While there has been responsible reporting of child abuse, there has also been an unfortunate amount of tabloid-type coverage, with much less follow-up when the truth comes out. At times, the mainstream media appears to go into a feeding frenzy in its search for lurid accusations. The press has usually given a great deal more coverage to the prosecution's point of view than that of the defendant accused of ritual abuse.

Daytime TV talk shows also feed the frenzy. Geraldo Rivera has produced several specials on Satanism. He considers himself an investigative journalist, but when interviewing Richard Ramirez, the "Nightstalker," a serial murderer in prison in California for killing several people, he listened wide-eyed to Ramirez's explanation for his crimes. "I killed for the Dark Lord. . . . He promised me dominion over 10,000 souls if I killed for him," the criminal raved while holding up his hand to the camera, showing a pentagram and devil's head tattooed on his left palm.

A responsible investigative journalist might have asked a question or two, such as "What does having dominion over 10,000 souls get you? Do they type? Do they do your laundry? Do they have a plan to get you out of prison? How can you tell that you have dominion over 10,000 souls?" But not Geraldo. He just stared in awe at the jerk he was giving national airtime to, as if he believed this guy was actually something other than a self-serving psychopath who felt like raping and killing some people and did.

In another "special," Geraldo interviewed some obviously mentally ill women who claimed they had been used as "breeders" for satanic cults. He never mentioned whether he asked any of them to be medically checked to see if they'd ever even been pregnant. Geraldo also raved on and on about the "proof" he had of the international satanic conspiracy. His proof—almost everyone he spoke to told him it didn't exist! That's proof, don'tcha know, either that the interviewees are in on it or that they are too afraid of those satanic folks to even talk about them.

Stung to the quick by criticism of his brand of television sideshow, Geraldo published a challenge to other TV talkshows to become more responsible in early 1996. Of course, he is not planning to implement the new guidelines until the fall, or at least not until after "sweeps week."

Mainstream publishers have also behaved irresponsibly by publishing as non-fiction the books from alleged survivors of cult abuse, and those written by therapists who treat them, either without doing the necessary background research to evaluate the claims or by simply accepting that recovered memories are a valid source of factual information with no physical evidence to support it.

These abuse stories are compelling! They are so awful, and so dramatic, that they can suck you right into their emotional center. However, they also sound a great deal like the spectral evidence used to convict witches in Salem, Massachusetts. Once you really understand what an urban myth is, you can spot them everytime.

Fundamentalist feminists and sexual panic

Let us not forget the fourth force behind the satanic ritual child abuse panic, the reactionary branch of the women's movement. Personified by *Ms. Magazine* and personalities such as Andrea Dworkin and Katherine MacKinnon, they appear to believe that most of women's problems are caused by men looking at pictures of naked women. The issue of *Ms.* with a child on the cover and the caption "Ritual Abuse—Believe It" was, in my opinion, a support of spectral evidence. Dworkin and MacKinnon, who enjoy a great deal of status and support within the feminist fundamentalist point of view, are against any sort of sexually explicit media; MacKinnon has written "If pornography is part of your sexuality, then you have no right to your sexuality," and Dworkin has written "Lesbian-written pornography . . . is an expression of self-hatred."

There is a huge battle going on within feminism around sexuality and personal identity for women. As the battle rages, more and more of the public dismiss feminism as irrelevant. Just as the earlier women's movement lost its focus on changing the status of women and sidetracked into the temperance movement, the current branch of the women's movement that gets the most press coverage and support has sidetracked into fighting smut and changing laws to "protect" women.

Feminist organizations such as Feminists for Free Expression, the Northwest Feminist Anti-Censorship Taskforce and even several of the larger state NOW organizations have publicly taken stands against the Mac-Dworkinites, but they get much less press coverage that the smut-chasers.

It is mainly women and children who are being abused, and/or jailed, by the current [sexual/satanic panic] hysteria.

How did it happen that a movement begun to assist women in achieving status and opportunity equal to men went bonkers over dirty pictures? It was simple. An alliance was formed between religious fundamentalists, who wanted to get rid of all sexual media, and feminists, who wanted to get rid of sexual media they felt degraded women.

This alliance enabled both groups to be taken much more seriously by the mainstream press, so they got a lot more coverage as each legitimized the other. Both liberal and conservative watchdogs who would ordinarily attack those suggesting such sweeping changes to the Constitution said nothing out of respect for the members of their own political camp who were involved. Unfortunately both groups were obsessed with sex and sexual media, which while entertaining to argue about will never change the real balance of power. The hubbub diverted public attention from any focus on real social change.

This alliance with the far right has changed feminism much more than vice versa and has moved fundamentalist feminism further from the concerns of most Americans.

There are a number of women, however, Susie Bright, Laura Antoniou, Dorothy Allison, Pat Califia, Carol Queen, Sallie Tisdale and Annie Sprinkle just to name a few, who are reclaiming their sexuality and declaring that sexually explicit media, porn if you prefer that term, is good in itself, and they refuse to apologize for writing it, enjoying it and defending it.

What is going on here?

In reading the writings of the antipornography feminists, the far right Christians, and the other antisex people, I am puzzled by their obsession with collecting examples of explicit depictions of disgusting sexual practices while claiming they are decrying other people's interest in explicit depictions of disgusting sexual practices. There is something very strange in the fundamentalist religious, feminist and other collections of sexually explicit media. Like the Meese Commission on Pornography, they appear to obsessively collect that which gives them the least pleasure and which upsets them the most. They then demand the rest of us look at this stuff and join them in their disgust. They claim they do it to protect others from the negative effects of this type of media. Reverend Wildmon has sent thousands of copies of homoerotic media though the mail nationwide in fundraisers asking for money to prevent this stuff from being available. Are these people an unconscious satire of themselves?

The perfect example of this is child pornography. Only a very small number of adults find explicit depictions of young children having sex erotic. A much larger group of adults find explicit depictions of teenagers having sex erotic, and until recently most states considered teens from around age 15 or 16 capable of consenting to sexual activity and marriage. In the name of protecting "children," which most of us would think of as the very young, from being sexually abused, explicitly depicted or being exposed to sexual information, the religious and feminist forces of conservatism have pressed for and succeeded in having the age of consent raised to age 18 in many states, and in making sexually explicit media more difficult to obtain.

Now this indeed creates more "child sexual abuse" and "child pornography," since sexual behavior and explicit media that were legal under the previous statutes are now illegal, and teenagers and adults now have less access to sexual media they find entertaining or sexual information that they may feel they need to make life decisions.

Since child pornography featuring young children is very rare, as there is such a small market for it, to find anything other than fantasy stories one would have to search relentlessly. So for years the U.S. government has been reproducing the child porn in its collection, and spending endless time and tax money to try to entice people to buy it, so it can then arrest the buyers. The laws against possession of child pornography do not apply to the government, and they are replicating it to protect us from it.

If recovered memories come to be widely accepted as proof in courts of law, anyone could be accused of anything.

The current media uproar of the moment is over "cyberporn." Quotes such as "At the click of a mouse button, explicit pornography is available to children" would be laughable if they were not fueling the attempt to control and censor the Internet. I invite anyone to jump aboard the "Information Superhighway" and see if you as an adult can do anything "at the click of a mouse button." It takes real expertise to find and display those naughty pictures, few of which are any different than what is widely available in magazines and are of less quality as the computer screen is inferior to print media. Most explicit sexual media costs money on the Internet, which would preclude children from purchasing it without their parents' credit cards. But in their war for the public attention, sex and danger sell a lot of magazines, newspapers and air-time.

Have these changes had any positive effect on the safety of children? Not in my opinion.

These forces, and the contradictions in all our feelings regarding sexuality, feed the generalized fear that we have for the safety of our children, ourselves and for the future of society as we know it. Like Desert Storm, and for some the O.J. Simpson trial, the satanic ritual abuse stories draw our attention until we cannot seem to look away or think clearly. They also create an instant stardom of a sort for those who come up with the most spectacular stories, and an acceptable reason ("I was abused as a child") for any sort of personal irresponsibility a person wishes to indulge in.

The real victims of satanic abuse

Many of those who speak out against the sexual/satanic panic are accused of being callous toward the suffering of women and children, of participating in their abuse by defending such things as the First Amendment to the Constitution or of being part of the satanic plot themselves. Most of the people who are prosecuting individuals and groups, pressing to have laws changed and learning to work with abused individuals would say that they are doing it to protect women and children. However, a look at the facts will show that it is mainly women and children who are being abused, and/or jailed, by the current hysteria.

Of the 132 people on a list of accused, naming only defendants in the bigger cases that get some public attention where there is very good evidence that no crime occurred, at least 55 can be identified as women; as some names are gender-neutral, the number of women may be larger.

As for the abuse of children, when an accusation is made that a child has been sexually abused, the child is interviewed 20 to 30 times. When the accusation includes ritual or satanic abuse, the number of interviews can double or triple. This interviewing could be considered a form of child abuse, particularly in those cases where it is probable that no abuse had actually occurred.

It is not that children should not be protected. It is absolutely necessary that children be protected. But are the actions being taken protecting children? Please do not think that such accusations could not happen to you. If recovered memories come to be widely accepted as proof in courts of law, anyone could be accused of anything, and since it is practically impossible to prove that something did not happen, what defense would be accepted? Many states have changed laws to enable anyone to charge another person with a crime that happened twenty or thirty years ago, long past the statute of limitations for the crime, by merely saying that the memory of it had been repressed and recently remembered.

The question is, who gains and who loses from these prosecutions, particularly the big scandalous ones that get a lot of press? And who is victimizing the children?

Most states have laws (because of CAPTA) making it impossible to recover damages from false accusations of child abuse, even if the accused can prove that the prosecution, or anyone, deliberately withheld information that would have cast doubt on the charges. Even if an accused person is acquitted, they seldom can recover either their reputation or their expenses. In *Satanism in American: How the Devil Got Much More than His Due*, by Shawn Carlson and Gerry O'Sullivan, it is estimated that by the late 1980s over $200 million had been spent by various levels of federal, state and local government and law enforcement to attempt to find evidence of satanic child abuse cults. Guess who is really picking up that tab?

Why do people make up these stories? Why would anyone publish a book saying such experiences are true when they are fiction? The writers of the satanic and recovered memory fiction won't say. Undoubtedly, some believe their stories to be true. As for the others, fame and fortune could be two reasons. Another reason is that first person "true" stories need not be as well written as fiction in order to sell. I would be less concerned about this whole issue if these satanic abuse accusations and recovered memories were not destroying people's lives, including those who believe it happened to them.

Possibly everyone has a fantasy "other" whose fault it is that the world is not going right. Have you stopped to think who yours might be? Maybe it is the Christians, or the feminists, the multinational corporations, the militia, the Democrats or Republicans, the immigrants, welfare recipients, the government—who do you blame for the problems of the world?

The next few years will probably see increasing craziness as all these forces build to the millennium. I fear many more people will be falsely accused and imprisoned before a return to rational standards is demanded in accusations and trials. We humans do not know how to get along respectfully in multicultural groups. Yet we are moving toward a world society. What are we going to do?

Internet Resources

An e-mail list is available for people interested in discussing and learning more about this social controversy. To subscribe to it, send email to witchhunt-subscribe@yahoogroups.com. You can also go to the website at http://groups/yahoo.com and sign on. Search for "witchhunt" if you are not already a member and subscribe. After you are accepted, you will be able to read the archives of the discussion.

Eric Krock's Stop Bad Therapy site: This site contains a wealth of information. www.stopbadtherapy.com.

Dean Tong's site which provides resource information and more for those unjustly accused of child abuse. His new book is due out in a August 2001—*ELUSIVE INNOCENCE: Survival Guide For The Falsely Accused* (Huntington House, 2001). Thanks for his help with this article: www.abuse-excuse.com.

False Allegations of Child Sexual Abuse Website: www.falseabuse.com.

Laura Pasley's Website: She originally "recovered" memories while spending several years in therapy, and is now a retractor, i.e. a person who has come to realize she was duped by her therapists. She sued, won several million dollars and is now committed to exposing this witchhunt: www.geocities.com/heartland/pointe/3171/.

The Ontario Centre for Religious Tolerance maintains a webpage which deals with ritual abuse, recovered memory and etc. for those who wish to learn more: www.religioustolerance.org.

8

Teen Satanists Are Rebelling Against the Dominant Culture

Kathleen S. Lowney

Kathleen S. Lowney is an associate professor of sociology at Valdosta State University in Georgia.

A study of a coven of teen Satanists reveals that although members of the coven tended to be marginalized members of society, they did not become Satanists to participate in major criminal activities. Instead, the group was formed to critique and rebel against the dominant culture, norms, and values of the teens' community. In the process, the teen Satanists formed close social bonds and developed a new self-identity. The coven was intensely opposed by the dominant culture.

Satanism has been much discussed of late, primarily by the popular media and less so by the scholarly community. A very few analysts have seen it as a nonthreatening new religious movement, one among many that have attracted members since the 1960s. Many more people have seen Satanism as an unhealthy, perhaps even criminal enterprise that hurts all those who encounter it. In this view, Satanists are likely to be child abusers, murderers, and substance abusers, and are constantly looking for others to harm or to recruit. Children and adolescents are the most vulnerable to the seduction of the Devil's grasp; thus the activity must be stopped to prevent further innocents from being led astray down the path to Hell.

Those who see Satanism as dangerous have described it as "a belief system that uses occult magic and employs ritual practices that constitute a travesty of Christianity" (Moriarty and Story 1990, 187). For these individuals, religion "refers to Judeo-Christian practices and belief system commonly associated with Western culture" (Moriarty and Story 1990, 187). Those who accept such a definition of Satanism are Christian evangelists (e.g., Larson 1989), ex-Satanists (e.g., Stratford [1987] 1991; Warnke

From "Teenage Satanism as Oppositional Youth Subculture," by Kathleen S. Lowney, *Journal of Contemporary Ethnography*, vol. 23, no. 4 (January 1995), pp. 453–84. Copyright © 1995 by Sage Publications, Inc. Reprinted by permission of Sage Publications, Inc.

1972), and many in the psychiatric community (e.g., Moriarty and Story 1990; Wheeler, Wood, and Hatch 1988). They hold that Satanists are dangerous people—to others, especially innocent children, and even to themselves. They regard them as mentally disturbed individuals, often addicted to drugs or sadistic sexual practices. The psychiatric description that Satanists are "dysfunctional" or "sick" comes almost entirely from three sources: hospitalized teenagers diagnosed as Satanic practitioners (Belitz and Schacht 1992; Bourget, Gagnon, and Bradford 1988; Moriarty and Story 1990; Steck, Anderson, and Boylin 1992), prisoners whose crimes were said to have been inspired by Satanism, and ex-Satanists, many of whom subsequently converted to Christianity. Those who hold to this explanation proclaim that American moral values (religious faith, family unity, etc.) are breaking down, and that Satanism has flourished in such a morally bankrupt social environment.

This construction of Satanism has been prominently expressed in popular media, especially on television talk shows.[1] Talk show hosts rely on psychiatric experts to explain the danger to Satanists and to those they might victimize. According to this explanation, the cause of these "sick" or deviant behaviors is the Satanic faith that practitioners espouse. The most common prescription is counseling (be it exit counseling [religious in nature] or psychotherapy). Therapeutic intervention is seen as the sole means of releasing the person from the Devil's grip (e.g., Rudin 1990; Speltz 1990; and Tennant-Clark, Fritz, and Beauvais 1989).

A social-scientific explanation

The other primary explanation is a more social-scientific one. Satanism is understood to encompass a range of beliefs and practices: it can be simply mislabeled youthful playfulness, or it can be a social movement that is seemingly harmless though often flamboyant (Richardson, Best, and Bromley 1991a), or it may even be the rationale for criminal behavior (Crouch and Damphousse 1992; Taub and Nelson 1993).

In the earliest sociological literature, Satanism, or more precisely, certain organized Satanic groups that Taub and Nelson (1993) called the Satanic Establishment, were seen to have "achieved a measure of social legitimation" (p. 525) in the American religious plurality. These groups contain adult, not juvenile members: Alfred (1976) found that the vast majority of members in the Church of Satan were "middle-class white people in their forties, thirties, and late twenties, including many professionals" (p. 194). Moody's (1974) study of the (Satanic) Church of the Trapezoid, and Bainbridge's study (1978) of The Power, a Satanic cult, also characterized their members as adults. These establishment groups had a cohesive theology and praxis, and did not involve themselves in criminal conduct, nor did their values differ significantly from those of many other American organizations (Taub and Nelson 1993).

Teens and Satanism

Recent sociological literature about Satanism has stressed a constructionist analysis of the moral panic created by claimmakers who advocated the psychiatric explanation (e.g., Forsyth and Olivier 1990; Lippert 1990;

Richardson, Best, and Bromley 1991a) rather than an analysis of actual practitioners. So much of our knowledge about teenagers involved in what popular culture calls Satanism stems from the work of folklorists. Ellis (1982–1983, 1991b) has argued that teenagers act out local legends by visiting "haunted" sites, a practice called legend-tripping. He stated (1991b) that legend-tripping frequently includes acts of deviant behavior such as graffiti spray-painting, breaking and entering abandoned churches, and vandalizing graveyards. This is not "real" Satanism but ostentation, the physical re-enactment of local legends. The role-playing done on these legend-trips is "the significant thing to the adolescent, and the legend serves mainly as an excuse to escape adult supervision, commit antisocial acts, and experiment illicitly with drugs and sex. Both legend and trip are ways of saying 'screw you' to adult law and order" (Ellis 1982–1983, 64). Ellis has argued that, given the hysteria instigated by the moral panic, law enforcement officers, educators, mental health professionals, and parents have overreacted and inappropriately labeled legend-trippers as Satanists. Ellis comes close to arguing that there is little actual Satanic religious behavior among adolescents; what seems visible is more often simply misunderstood, mislabeled legend-trip activity.

The "disturbed" explanation given by the mental health professionals, the folklorists' legend-tripping explanation, and to a lesser extent the constructionist literature that explores the anti-Satanist claim-making agenda, assume that there is a dominant culture against which individual young adults are reacting with their "Satanic" behaviors. These explanations privilege this dominant culture, arguing that "healthy" teens would not feel alienated from peers, parents, community, and that these adolescents eventually will stop rebelling and join the "real," adult world. This theoretical privileging of one culture accomplishes two things: first, it keeps the analysis focused on "bad" or "sick" *individuals* rather than on the level of the social group, and second, it does not allow for an analysis of teenage Satanists as *social critics* of the dominant culture.[2]

The voices of adolescent Satanists are absent from the sociological literature. Gaines (1990) briefly discussed what she called "Satanteens," with little analysis of their beliefs. Crouch and Damphousse (1992) discussed "self styled" or "youth subculture" Satanists. They assume that all such Satanists "sometime engage in activities that are not only bizarre by conventional standards but also criminal" (p. 5). They offer no firsthand data to support this claim. Crouch and Damphousse agree with Taub and Nelson (1993) that youthful Satanists should be classified as members of the Satanic Underground, with its "reputed participation in antisocial or criminal behavior. Activities of these individuals or groups are less structured and lack the organizational dimensions of the Satanic Establishment" (p. 525).

Here again, theoretical dichotomies such as "Satanic Establishment" versus "Satanic Underground" are too simplistic. Critical questions must be asked about these descriptions of adolescent Satanism: "underground" to whom? "antisocial" according to whose moral perspective? "conventional" according to whose viewpoint? "less structured" according to whose standards? Terms such as these also imply a privileged position, in this case by the sociological analyst. These would not be the terms used by many youthful Satanists to describe their own activities.

The Coven

Ethnographic accounts of modern-day adolescent Satanists are needed, including accounts of Satanists who are not hospitalized in a psychiatric facility, and accounts that give participants' explanation for their religious behaviors. In this article I analyze five years of fieldwork with the Coven, a Satanic adolescent subculture in a Southern community I shall call "Victory Village." What emerges from these data is far removed from the psychiatric interpretation. Although it is a "view from below"—the explanation constructed by the teenage Satanists themselves—it is *not* an examination of the Taub and Nelson's "Satanic Underground." The Coven did not participate in major criminal activities.

What the Coven did was to present a critique of the dominant culture of Victory Village. Thus the Coven is yet another example of how youth subcultures can challenge the hegemony of the dominant culture (e.g., Brake 1980; Cohen 1980; Fox 1987; Gaines 1990; Hebdige 1979[3]). Their subcultural opposition operated on several levels simultaneously: first, it was *collective* articulation of a cultural critique; second, it allowed them to establish and maintain a new self-concept; and third, it provided a symbolic challenge to the dominant culture's value system.

What the Coven did was to play with the social categories and boundaries of Victory Village. These were so accepted by many in the community that they had become almost imperceptible over time. The Coven made visible the dominant culture's valued statuses as it simultaneously rejected them. But its rejection of the dominant culture antagonized Victory Village.

To understand what the Coven got from its Satanic faith—even in the face of such rejection—requires listening to the story of Victory Village from these adolescents' perspective. I tell their story as they told it to me, first by explaining the dominant culture as they saw it and then by describing their critique of that culture. In particular, I focus on their development of a Satanic style as an expression of their opposition to Victory Village.

Method

I have been on my college's Speaker's Bureau—a faculty list of those willing to speak to the community on topics related to their expertise—since I came to this institution in 1987. I was listed as an expert on "new religious movements/cults," because my doctoral dissertation focused on a well-known new religion. One day in March of 1988, three calls came in to the Public Relations Department and were referred to me. The calls either asked me about, or informed me of, Satanic activities in neighboring high schools. The first and third calls were from Christian ministers who wanted me to speak to their youth groups about what was happening. The second call was from an employee of a nearby bookstore who knew of me, notifying me that during the last six weeks there had been over thirty-five special orders placed for *The Satanic Bible* (LaVey 1969). That very day I began interviewing members of the press, law enforcement, and school systems for their perspective on what was occurring. These interviews, plus background reading on Satanism (academic and popular), took up the bulk of my research time for the next two months. I also went to one of the youth groups, less as an expert than as a listener. From those Christian young adults I gathered not just names of possible Coven members, but also learned more about their behaviors and favorite hangouts.

For the next several months, I frequented locations where, according to the Christian youths, the Coven met. Primarily this meant going to the mall on Friday nights and observing until it closed. From the non-Satanist youth's descriptions of the Coven's style, I was able to identify possible members quite easily. Through background interviews with youth ministers and others, I learned of more names; sometimes members even were pointed out to me. Thus even before contact was made with the Coven, I was able to begin to sort out membership status and style matters. I sat and observed numerous interactions of the Coven while members played games, as well as their interactions with non-Satanic youth, the shopping public, food court workers, and mall security guards. Initially I observed from a distance; over time I would chat with some members and other young adults at the arcade. I was becoming a "social fixture" at the mall. These observations gave me some idea of the group's norms, structure, and argot prior to the interviewing phase.

Over time, Satanic beliefs, practices, and rituals were constructed by members to . . . critique the dominant culture, and . . . create a new self-identity.

Simultaneously, I began visiting other locations I heard the Coven discuss—in particular local bridges—but I went on Friday afternoons or Saturday mornings, when it was less likely that I would meet the group, because the Coven visited them after the mall closed on Friday nights. These visits gave me some sense of the less public activities of the Coven. I took photographs of these sites when I found evidence of Coven activities: Satanic graffiti, such as "Playing with black magic is fun" or Satanic pentagrams painted on trees to mark the way into a rural meeting site; non-Satanic graffiti but signed with Coven nicknames, such as one male who often went by the name of "Casper." He tended to paint "Casper loves." Not only could I trace his whereabouts with these messages, but I could also follow his romantic history as well.

I continued to talk with Christian youth groups; from them I realized that I needed to know more about high school culture. Therefore I continued to visit the mall and video arcade; I interviewed local merchants (bookstore, music store, alternative clothing stores, etc.) I also began to observe the areas of the high school parking lots when school was getting out.

After about one year, I became known as an "expert" in Satanism. This status opened some new research opportunities. I was given permission to attend an Occult Crime Workshop for Georgia law enforcement officers. I was the only non-law enforcement person present during the three day workshop. The workshop fit the model described by Hicks (1991a, 1991b, personal communication): a law enforcement officer presented a great deal of data—mostly clips from television talk shows. His analytical framework blended the psychiatric explanation—"Satanists were sickies"—with a heavy dose of conservative Christianity. He showed little understanding of other religions (confusing Santeria with Voodoo, for instance) and labeled any new religious movement, such as the Unification Church, as Satanic. Claims about the growing number of Satanic or occult crimes were repeatedly made, with no evidence presented to support them. While there, I interviewed five police officers from various jurisdictions in Georgia, as well as local officers who also attended the workshop.

Coven members grew increasingly hostile to the outside world as they saw it, in particular due to the fact that the Coven felt [the community] would never change.

Throughout the course of the research, I was invited to attend or to lecture at workshops on Satanism for social workers (local and state level), probation and parole officers (state level), and educators (local level). During these meetings I conducted interviews, primarily with those people who stayed afterward to discuss specific work-related incidents. I have interviewed local (Georgia) television reporters and print journalists, and I had several telephone interviews with a Florida television anchor who ran a week-long special on the evening news about teenage Satanism. Although certainly not systematic, it can be argued that the interviews with these professionals might well represent concerns about the "worst" cases of alleged Satanism among Georgia and Florida teenagers.

By mid-1989, some Coven members agreed to be interviewed. This took a long time to arrange due to ethical concerns about studying minors involved in Satanism without the informed consent of their parents or guardians.[4] More males than females agreed to one-on-one interviews, although there were several opportunities for informal group discussions (especially about makeup) with females during observations at the mall. Interviews were often unplanned. Twice members or former members showed up at my faculty office ready to talk.[5] I learned to keep a notebook, camera, and tape recorder with me. Interviews were most often unstructured. I let the member lead our discussion, and asked questions mostly for clarification. During later interviews, and only with certain subjects, I was more directive and brought up topics for discussion.

Interviews

All the young adults interviewed were involved with the Coven, though membership status varied. I interviewed four very active members; two less active members; and two ex-members. From mid-1989 to 1991, I conducted over fifteen interviews; they ranged from just under one hour to several hours in length. Most often the interviews occurred in a setting chosen by the Coven member. This often meant that interviews were done outdoors, sometimes while sitting on the hood of a car, often with a car stereo playing in the background.

Interactions with the Coven, especially at first, were sometimes problematic. They were not sure how to treat me and how much they could trust me. I was a teacher, yet not *their* teacher; I was an adult yet I had no real authority over them. Some of this awkwardness disappeared during the observational stage, especially after the Coven knew who I was and became used to me. We eventually negotiated a "friend role" (Fine 1987) that was comfortable for them and for me. I dressed casually during observations; I deliberately purchased compact discs at the music store for personal enjoyment when in the presence of the Coven; some members had much to say about my taste in music. These behaviors allowed interactions to occur that facilitated the friendship role. Perhaps the two most disconcerting issues that emerged during the research were religion and confidentiality. For eight years I have worn a Christian cross. It had become such a part of my presentation of self that I often forgot it was there. Coven members, once they felt comfortable around me, sometimes commented about it. Because I asked them about their jewelry and why they wore it, I responded in kind. Often this led into conversations about religion. I was expected to participate, not just observe, and I did, sometimes sharing moments in my life that were either religious highs or lows. These conversations were quite comfortable for me. Where religion became problematic was when adults who knew I was studying the Coven expected that my research goal was to talk members out of Satanism. In particular, some Christian adults felt strongly that I was letting them and/or the community down if I was not deconverting the teens. I was not always successful at explaining that deconversion was never my goal. Several times these adults asked me if I was a secret Satanist—Why else was I not trying to get the kids out of the Devil's grip?

The Coven was seen as threatening to the community's social harmony.

Although religious issues were more problematic between myself and those outside the Coven, confidentiality was more difficult to negotiate with the Coven. As the research progressed, I learned that children of social acquaintances were involved. These teens were concerned that I would report their activities (especially Coven membership, sneaking out of the house, and underage drinking) to parents/guardians. As trust built up and they learned that I would not, this declined as an issue.

Only one other issue ever proved problematic—underage consumption of alcohol. For the most part, members never drank in my presence, or if they did, they were of legal age. Twice I was asked to provide alcohol for a gathering and both times I refused. This refusal had less to do with my concern that I would be stepping over an "ethical line in the sand" than that this could have led to my arrest for supplying alcohol to minors. Both times the request was withdrawn after my refusal, or turned into a joke that, "Oh yea, she doesn't drink . . . she's allergic to alcohol . . . she wouldn't know what the fuck to get anyway." The use of humor (by them or me) allowed the role of friend to be maintained.

During the years of data-gathering, over thirty-five young adults had at least some involvement with the Coven. Three were members throughout the entire study and to my knowledge considered themselves Satanists by the time I concluded my research, though they were no longer active in the Coven because they were in colleges away from home. All were White; almost all were from middle- or upper-middle-class families. A third of the membership was female; a female was the charismatic leader for over two years.

The dominant culture

The acquisition of culture by any particular individual is a complex interactive process, mediated both by other individuals (parents, peers, siblings) and social institutions (religion, schools, mass media). A culture, however dominant it may be, "is not uniformly spread throughout a social system" (Fine and Kleinman 1979, 1); rather, culture is internalized to different degrees due to sociocultural variables such as social class, race, sex, and age. Victory Village's dominant culture, as it was internalized by its adolescents, can be summed up in one word—football. The high school team consistently ranked among the top twenty-five high school football teams in the nation. The team boasted a record that included two national championships and numerous state championships; in the last four years the team was featured on at least two national news programs.[6]

This football culture created multiple status hierarchies within the student body. From the Coven's perspective, these hierarchies amounted to an unmentioned but understood categorization of the entire student body. Richard, a non-Satanist high school junior, described the social structure of Victory Village High School this way:

> Well, here's how it is. . . . There's the jocks and their ladies—
> they're on the top. Then their flunkies, cheerleaders, and the
> band. All *they* do is make the football jocks look good. . . .
> Then there's the geeks, oh, I mean the greeks. They're rich
> and White and let everyone know it. . . . Then the acade-
> mics—yeah, that's most of us over there—study, work, go to
> [football] games if we want to, ya know, regular folks. . . .
> Then there's the others, you know, the artsy types—they're
> odd, but they have God-given talent, I guess. . . . There's the
> freaks—druggies, or just the odd ones, they just don't fit in
> anywhere.

Although these groups tend toward intragroup activities, Fine and Kleinman (1979) has written that "it is erroneous to conceive of group members as interacting exclusively with each other. Small groups are connected with many other groups through a large number of interlocks, or social connections" (p. 8). So too, in Victory Village high schools, the organization of the schools forced a limited amount of mixing, primarily in classrooms, the parking lots, and lunchrooms. The groups also interacted outside of the high schools, in particular at the favorite adolescent leisure activity sites such as the shopping mall and theaters.

One of the ways groups differentiate themselves is through constructing unique styles. Style is

> the expressive elements used by an actor in his way of act-
> ing upon the world. This includes the way he organizes his

experiences, his perceptions, and his cognitions at the psychological level, as well as his appearance, bearing, and life style. . . . Style indicates who one is, and where one is at—it indicates identity in a particular way (Brake 1974, 185).

Even dominant groups developed particular styles. The football players dressed conspicuously, in football jerseys, school colors, and sweats. They used a specialized argot to talk about their games, training procedures, and opponents. Cheerleaders also had a particular presentation of self—appropriate makeup, hairstyles, and weight—as well as a language of cheers and planning activities for the athletes. Band members had props such as uniforms and instruments, which readily identified them. Thus each group developed a unique style that both bonded members to each other and served to socially locate them.

Although these status hierarchies divided the student body, there was a unifying force in the high school, indeed in the community. Christian faith was normative in Victory Village. A woman, shopping in the local mall, expressed this "social fact" to two Coven females, when she yelled at them:

> Okay, you've made your point; you don't like my religion [the woman was wearing a Christian cross and had just come out of a Christian bookstore]. But this is a *Christian* community—we don't want you around either. So go, why don't you? Just leave, go somewhere, maybe Atlanta, some big city where there are more like you . . . just go, before my daughter gets to high school next year.

Christianity permeated Victory Village. Prayers were said before football games. Weekly church attendance was customary among both adolescents and adults. Symbols of the faith were very visible; Christian crosses were commonplace as jewelry, especially among females. Most athletes and cheerleaders belonged to Christian organizations. Living the Christian lifestyle, as preached to adolescents, involved self-control of the body to be an excellent athlete, sexually chaste, and physically attractive. Thus membership in the larger body of the faithful to some degree mitigated the status divisions in Victory Village High School: adolescents saw each other frequently in church.

Socially marginalized

Nevertheless, some students were socially marginalized. Mark, an ex-member of the theater group and the most prolific of the Coven's graffiti artists, can serve as an example:

> I knew they didn't want me in class. They all sat together. . . . I let 'em . . . What the hell did I care anyway? They never would have talked to me anyway. I made 'em uncomfortable—if they couldn't see me, they could go on the way they always were—praying a lot, yet being god damn mean to anyone below them. . . . I let 'em think they were better than me, . . . 'cuz dammit, I knew the *truth.*

The "truth," for Mark, was Satanism. He described an incremental

conversion process, whereby social bonds developed both prior to and simultaneously with his conversion to this Satanic group.[7]

> I never felt accepted at this school. Always felt different—
> sometimes that hurt, sometimes I was glad to be different.
> Who'd want to be like those motherfucking hypocritical
> Christians? . . . Love your enemies—ya, let's see that attitude
> on the football field some Friday night! . . . Then I noticed
> her one day, at lunch I think. She was an outsider too—
> could see that by her hair. But something was different. . . .
> She seemed proud of it. I began to find out about her; hang
> around her. She fascinated me, especially her appearance. . . .
> Everyday was something different . . . She seemed exciting,
> daring others to challenge her. . . . So I got to know her,
> Zena. She was proud, proud of her uniqueness. I wanted that
> too—to feel better, no, *good* about myself. Don't remember
> just how it happened—maybe I was drunk when I finally did
> it—I finally asked her about it. And she showed me her *truth*.
> So I borrowed it [*The Satanic Bible*] for awhile. . . . If it worked
> for her, gave her all that fucking air of being above those
> shitty athletes and rich snobs . . . well, I wanted it too.

Mark's story was typical. All of the Coven's membership shared this
extremely marginalized social location at the high school. Many had
been members of the "artistic" group—already a lower status group, but
they did not want to continue interacting with that group. Chris, a Coven
member for three months, said, "I got tired of all the rehearsals. I had better things to do with my time." So over a period of months, the Coven
was formed. It created a mechanism to *decrease* individual marginality by
inventing a new solidarity for its members, yet in so doing, its members
actually *increased* their social isolation by espousing a Satanic idioculture
(Fine 1982) and style that is not the normative culture of Victory Village.

The Coven's critique of the dominant culture

Any group interacts with others over the course of time. These interactions serve critical functions in the construction of group beliefs, practices, and ideology. The marginalized status of some high school students
in Victory Village, and their hostility to the in groups who had higher status in the school and community, led to the formation of the Coven.
Over time, Satanic beliefs, practices, and rituals were constructed by
members to serve two main purposes: first, to critique the dominant culture, and second, to create a new self-identity. As the Coven met these
goals, it further marginalized its members from other students and the
community. Coven members grew increasingly hostile to the outside
world as they saw it, in particular due to the fact that the Coven felt Victory Village would never change. Coven members were not able to fit into
the social structure of the high schools, no matter how hard they may
have attempted to do so. At some point, they had decided to stop trying.
Chris, one of the more visible male members, with his rock 'n roll t-shirts
and his shoulder-length hair, said:

> Yeah, I know there's fucking no chance of changing this

fucking town, [long pause] or even the damned school. But that doesn't mean I should just roll over and die—I am *here*, and so long as I can dress this way, think this way . . . then they will *have* to deal with me, with us [the Coven]. It's fun to see them look scared, look the other way when I come down the hall. . . . Don't tell me I don't have power. So long as I'm in the Coven, so long as I believe, I have *lots* of power—least to rattle their chains. Not sure can ask for more.

This hostility became channeled into a streetwise analysis of the dominant culture; in other words, the Coven settled on the role of social critic. Its mere visual presence was challenging to some in the community, even *prior* to their understanding the group's religious convictions. To those who knew this, too, the Coven was seen as threatening to the community's social harmony. And the Coven perceived this. Mark, a long-time member and sometimes leader, said:

I know lots of people in this fucking community wish we would disappear, or worse yet, be shipped off to [a local psychiatric hospital]. Too damned bad. . . . we're not going anywhere. I'm not sick . . . least not the way *they* mean it. I'm fucking sick of always being put down 'cuz I don't play football. Well too damned bad. Why is chasing a fucking ball up and down a field such a fucking god-given talent in this community? If I did that, coach says I could be important. Well, hell, *I am important*, dammit even though I fucking can't play football, *don't want to* play football. And if they don't see it, my friends [the Coven] do. We know we're important, see, if nothing else, we make *them* feel better about themselves . . . They can pray for us [laughter]. Like I need their motherfucking prayers. . . . Their God is weak. He can't even make [the county high school football] team win, even when they pray before a game . . . and they think He will save the world, save them? Hell no. . . . God dammit, Satan is all power; so am I. I want nothing to do with *them*, the adults who run this shitty place, nor their fucking kids who prance around the field or cheer on 'their team.' No thanks, I will make my own way. . . . don't want to live like them, no way. Don't want to look like 'em, talk like 'em. . . . I don't want to be one of *them*, fucking never do I.

The Coven, like many subcultures, found its role, its cohesiveness in social criticism of the dominant culture from which it felt rejected. Lacking the social power to change that culture, Coven members chose to change themselves as a statement to Victory Village. Brake (1980, vii) has written that

subcultures arise as attempts to resolve collectively experienced problems arising from the contradictions in the social structure, and that they generate a form of collective identity from which an individual identity can be achieved outside that ascribed by class, education, and occupation. This is nearly always a temporary solution, and in no sense is a real material solution, but one which is solved at the cultural level.

Creating a Satanic culture

And so the Coven members changed. Members created a Satanic subculture that diverged in both normative, cognitive, and behavioral aspects from the dominant culture of Victory Village. What the Coven created was a deliberate inversion of its perception of the dominant culture.

In particular, the Coven reversed what it perceived as the dominant culture's organization of space and time. The Coven chose to have its ritual sabbats[8] on Friday evenings, after the mall closed and at the same time as football games. "We try and get away from town, from the ass-kissing athletes playing their fucking games; that's where we do our thing." The Coven met in remote rural areas of the county. Their favorite ritual sites were bridges.[9] Although there were theological reasons for this,[10] there were other advantages. "We choose places that are one way in and one way out. That way we can see if anyone is coming and can stop the ritual. Our religion is for *us*, not just for anyone who wants to watch." In particular, the Coven kept a watchful eye out for law enforcement officers who might try to stop gatherings.[11]

By choosing remote rural sites for their rituals, the Coven acted out a central part of their oppositional subculture. Brake (1980, 35) has argued, "Physical space is not merely a simple territorial imperative, but symbolic of a whole life-style." Many of the bridges that the Coven used for ritual activity were in poor structural condition or actually closed to traffic. The Coven saw this as important. Mark best expressed this to me one night as he drew a map to one of the most remote Coven meeting sites.

> Our religion is about tearing down social lies and pointing out the truth, or as LaVey says, "Religion must be put to the question. No moral dogma must be taken for granted—no standard of measurement deified. There is nothing inherently sacred about moral codes. Like the wooden idols of long ago, they are the work of human hands, and what man has made, man can destroy!" We go to places that are in a state of decay—to show that the town is too!

During these nighttime rituals, the Coven seemed to choose a state of nature over the dominant Christian culture. The faraway bridge sites allowed them to be in touch with nature. The Coven saw itself as a small group operating in darkness, ritually illuminated by sacred candles and a campfire, calling forth demons to do its bidding. "We like the dark while they sit in the fucking stadium, lit up like a Christmas tree." Simultaneous with the Coven's sabbats, other teens were sitting in the "sacred center" of the football stadium, lit by artificial lights, collectively acting out the social norms of civil Christianity—to win the athletic contest, to "win" the right high school member of the opposite sex's attention, to be a success at the "game of life," so that they could reside in Heaven forever.

These two ideologies also disagreed about temporality. Christianity has a linear sense of time—it holds that all events, in both history and personal biography, will culminate in the end time, the Second Coming of Jesus Christ. All phenomena led to this one salvific event. For Christians, therefore, all time has a *future* emphasis. Believers orient their actions toward this ultimate goal; to live with little or no sin is to look forward to the Second Coming with joy instead of dread. Football athletes, cheerleaders, and the band practice for next games or the next season. For the Coven, there was no ultimate goal toward which time was oriented. Rather, Satanists lived in and for the present.

> Life is the great indulgence—death, the great abstinence. Therefore, make the most of life—HERE AND NOW! There is no heaven of glory bright, and no hell where sinners roast. Here and now is our day of torment! Here and now is our day of joy! Here and now is our opportunity! Choose ye this day, this hour, for no redeemer liveth! (LaVey, 62).

Following LaVey, the Coven did not divide social reality into past, present, and future. There was only the present. Alice, a member for just several months, nevertheless was able to articulate this part of the Coven's worldview: "What I want now, is what I want. If my desires change, it is because there is a new now."

This disparity between their views of temporality only deepened the rift between the two worldviews. The Satanists could not comprehend living life toward a future heavenly goal that one might not even attain, while Christians considered the Satanists' emphasis on fulfilling one's desires in the present as hedonistic and self-indulgent, if not sinful.

Thus the two worldviews clashed; their theologies were antithetical. Christian deportment, success in relationships and on the football field—these were the dominant culture's values internalized by Victory Village's adolescents. But the Coven rejected these values, choosing instead to pray to Satan, living for the moment and for self. Although Coven membership fluctuated over the years, its theology remained relatively constant. The Coven was theologically eclectic, using *The Satanic Bible* (1969) and several other books, such as *The Necronomicon* (1980) as a basic framework. Here too, the Coven saw itself as opposing Christian reliance upon only one sacred text. Mark, a member for over sixteen months at the time of our interview, said, "We don't have to be tied to just one book, written ages ago. No words in red for us, we interpret the [Satanic] Bible as we see it. It speaks to me differently each fucking day. And I just live it out."

Music

Thus personal experience was another theological source. Coven members brought to sabbat what was happening in their lives and the group ritually processed these life events. Several kinds of rituals were held; the most common involved members coming together at an isolated site, saying a few prayers to Satan, having a bonfire, drinking beer and wine coolers, criticizing Victory Village, and listening to rock music. Music offered both a way to ventilate emotions and to bond. "[M]usic is important because it articulates aspects of kids' lives, at a real or fantasy level" (Brake 1980, 157). As Mark said, "Like, I've had a shitty day. I'll go to sabbat, and be able to work through it all. Often I can't put it into words, but I'll play a song that says it all. Everyone understands then. I'm not too good with words, anyway."

The Coven's musical tastes shifted constantly. Their heavy metal favorites alternated between Megadeth, Motley Crue, Poison, Metallica, Guns and Roses, Ozzie Osbourne, and Anthrax; yet some members also like rap music and country songs.[12] More rarely "top 40" music could be heard from their portable stereo headsets. When questioned about this eclectic musical range, Chris, a guitar player himself, reported, "Yeah, I like metal music best. . . . guitars wailing. But mostly, it's what is being said. If it's bitching about the fucking world we've inherited, then I will probably like it. . . . but once and a while, I like a love song too." Coven members discussed both the structure of the music (guitar solos, etc.) and the lyrics. They seemed very aware of the lyrics, often interpreting them for me. In this, the Coven diverged from some of the findings in the literature about adolescents and heavy metal music (e.g., Prinksy and Rosenbaum 1987).

Sex rituals

Music was also a critical component of what the Coven called its "sex rituals."[13] The Coven enjoyed discussing these rituals in a vague and secretive fashion in front of outsiders, particularly high school teachers, as a way of, as Alice put it, "shaking up the establishment." For instance, Zena, the charismatic leader, was known by the ritual name, The Sex Goddess. This Satanic name was often "dropped" before nonmembers (especially teachers) in an attempt to confound, embarrass, and worry the larger social world. And it worked. One local teacher called me after hearing such a conversation. "All they do is have sex. Sex and Satan. That's all they write about in my class. I'm worried about them." Coven followers often laughed at the consternation their supposed sexual antics created. And yet despite their nomenclature, these rituals did not, to my knowledge, involve sexual intercourse. The sexual innuendos, however, clearly functioned as a source of power over nonmembers.

Most often these sex rituals involved the working of spells, often based on the sex chapter from *The Satanic Bible* (LaVey 1969), which focused on one member's sexual desire for someone else (either a member or a nonmember) and the spiritual mechanisms needed to accomplish that romantic goal. Spells tended to be highly personal in nature, composed by the individual but shared in the ritual context of sabbat. Members supported one another throughout the duration of the spell through prayer, conversation, listening to music as ritual activity, and confidence-building behaviors. Spells detailed the magical steps necessary to requite one's sexual desire for the other person. Mark shared a version of his spell for getting the girl of his dreams to go to a prom with him.

1. Pray to Satan about this every day. Ask for his guidance and support.
2. Change pattern of walking in the hallways in order to come into contact with the girl.
3. Begin to make eye contact with her.
4. Borrow/steal something of hers [a pen].
5. Talk to her, initially about inconsequential things.
6. Talk to her about Satanism and how Satan is the most important

person in his life, forever.
7. Use the personal object ritually to connect her to him forever. [This involved tying her pen to a pen of his. He carried them around for over two weeks.]
8. Eventually, ask her to the prom.

For each step in the spell, he had specific "Satanic prayers," which were to be repeated several times a day for the magic to become efficacious. These prayers consisted of poems that he had written, lyrics from love songs, passages from LaVey and other Satanic works about sex and love, and even a smattering of Emily Dickinson, whom he was studying in school. These prayers were the way he motivated himself to carry out these eight steps. The Coven provided a system of social and liturgical support for Mark; at least three sex rituals occurred during this two-week process. The sex rituals were collective encouragement—the prayers were heard by all; members supported Mark in his quest for a closer relationship with the female in question.

Through this ritual process, Mark structured his interactions with the female. He slowly progressed from being near her, to conversation, and he hoped, to a dating relationship. Slowly he gained enough confidence to approach this particular female (who was a fringe member of the group) and ask her out. By selecting a female who was at least somewhat familiar with Satanism, he further reduced his chances of romantic failure.

He reported that the ritual was a success, of a sort. The female did agree to go to the prom with him. However, he claimed to have had a miserable time. She "dressed up"; that is to say, she wore a prom dress, whereas Mark wore his typical attire, jeans and a heavy metal t-shirt. From that moment on, they seemed to have nothing in common. The date was "a motherfucking disaster." When asked to give a theological explanation for the apparent failure of his spell, Mark initially said that he had "just picked the wrong fucking broad to work it on." When he continued, "I guess she just wasn't really committed to my god. He [Satan] showed me that by getting us together, and then having her go *Christian* on me. Think she was a cheerleader or something." Neither Mark nor members in the Coven doubted their deity nor their belief system; the failure was due to inconsistent human followers. "I thought she was a true believer. But when I saw her all dressed up, I knew she wasn't. She wasn't as attractive to me then. . . . I had to keep asking myself *why* I had wanted to date her."

The Coven saw itself as a small group operating in darkness, ritually illuminated by sacred candles and a campfire, calling forth demons to do its bidding.

The Coven discussed this spell and its aftermath for some time, both in and out of Mark's presence. Eventually members constructed an explanation of what happened: Mark was being too "like them" (the Christians, the athletes) for even wanting to go to the prom, for wanting to date. This prom date entered into the group's folklore; five respondents told me some version of this story. In the social history of the Coven, this sex ritual concretized opposition to dyadic relationships, for they reflected all that was "bad" about the "others." From this point on, the Coven became an extended friendship network, but it did not condone dating relationships. To be dating was to be, in Alice's words, "a fucking cheerleader or at least acting like one." Thus the Coven's belief system was constructed so as to be flexible enough to allow members to view so-called "failures" as partial successes. These successes only further reinforced their Satanic, oppositional belief system.

This particular date/ritual was central to the Coven's subculture for yet another reason. It served as a "triggering event" (Fine 1982, 55) for the development of a normative style. Thereafter, the Coven standardized what was and was not acceptable clothing for its members. Whatever "the Christians," the athletes, or the cheerleaders wore was unacceptable.

Satanic style

The Coven recognized civil Christianity's control of the body for social purposes and explicitly rejected it. Coven members not only did not participate in the male athleticism and female presentation of self described above, they deliberately ridiculed it. Coven males laughed at the "jocks" who spent time working out in a gym. This stress on athleticism robbed them, in the Coven's mind, of time for more enjoyable activities. Male members took pride in not looking athletic. Steven, tall, thin, with his hair flowing loosely about his shoulders, told me, "I don't want anyone to confuse me with *them;* I look different, I look like I want to look." For Coven males, this style entailed consistently wearing black clothing, often heavy metal t-shirts, and long hair, pulled back in a pony-tail. Ed, a clerk at the local mall who frequently interacted with Coven members, referred to the Coven's male members as "throw-backs to the sixties." During the first few months of existence, members wore black trenchcoats with the word Megadeth (the Coven's favorite heavy metal band at that time) on the back. This apparel was even more striking given that the trenchcoats were worn in weather well above seventy degrees.

Coven women, however, showed the most visible opposition to "the other way." For almost 14 months, two young women wore solid black clothing. For much of the same time, they wore black nail polish as well. However, this was not the most obvious stylistic shift. Zena, for well over a year, changed her appearance on an almost daily basis. She would dye her hair different shades; her favorites were fluorescent colors. Each day her newly colored hair would be sculpted into a unique design. Mark, who first learned of the Coven after speaking to Zena regarding her hair, explained: "To make such a drastic change everyday made the artificiality of the whole thing [appearance and presentation of self] so apparent to us. She was trying to ridicule their focus on self by overidentifying with it." However, Zena's most obvious flaunting of norms came when she settled on one particular hairstyle. She dyed her hair white, with a strip of black extending from ear to ear across the back of her head and another strip from forehead to neck. What she had created on her head was an upside down Christian cross. She quite consciously reversed symbols in an attempt to articulate her own theology. Over the next few months, this hairstyle became popular with other female members. Although not all the high school, let alone the community of Victory Village recognized the symbolism of the upside down cross, the difference in presentation of self alone, was enough to be labeled as deviant. Those who recognized her hairstyle as a symbolic expression of her belief system were quite shocked. While observing the Coven at the local shopping mall one evening, I overheard someone tell her that "God would never forgive her" for what she was proclaiming through her hairstyle.

The Coven enjoyed discussing [sex] rituals in a vague and secretive fashion in front of outsiders . . . as a way of . . . "shaking up the establishment."

Makeup also served to emphasize the Coven's defiance of the norms of Victory Village. Spurning makeup styles taught in fashion magazines, many female Coven members wore a very white foundation, black or dark purple eyeshadow, black blush, and either black or deep purple lipstick. Members reported that they enjoyed these colors. "The goal of makeup shouldn't be about attracting boys, but being true to oneself, being faithful to Him [Satan]." The females viewed their presentation of self as symbolic affiliation with and membership in the Truth that Satan represented. Thus Alice, who wore not just purple blush, but for a brief time also wore a small hand-drawn Satanic pentagram near the outer corner of one eye, reported that, "I wear my makeup to say that I love Satan, just as *she* [one of the cheerleaders at the high school] wears her little gold cross to say that she is a Christian. Only hers is wrong; mine's right." Some female members admitted to "devouring [women's] magazines." They spent time learning what style (clothes, hair, makeup) was in fashion in order to reverse it. In this they were like some punk subcultures who have been studied (Fox 1987). Travers (1982) has argued that punkers "do know the ritual idiom that they violate, and in fact they know it in very fine detail because all their public life is lived in the narrow ground between normal appearances and illegal appearances" (p. 281).

Jewelry

Many Coven members flaunted their opposition to Victory Village in yet another symbolic way. They wore jewelry that advertised their religious worldview. Some Coven females and one male would wear an upside down Christian cross as an earring. This was an obvious inversion of Christian symbolism. However, other members chose to be more subtle, buying a set of tragedy and comedy mask stick pins. However, they would only wear the tragedy one. Even this more subtle component of their Satanic style drew comments. I witnessed two Coven females buying such pins. They first asked the clerk if the set could be broken up—they "only wanted to buy one of them." The clerk, nodding her head sympathetically, said, "I understand . . . who would want to wear the depressing one, with the sad face, after all?" She seemed shocked when the members said, "We would, that's the fucking one we wanted to get." The purchase complete, the females opened their packages and threw the comedy pin away. The clerk stared after them, shaking her head and muttering about "they're trouble."

So the Coven flaunted their theological differences with the surrounding society through a new style. By changing their presentation of
self, they literally embodied their change of social allegiance away from
the community's standards toward those of their own making. Like punk
styles before it, the Coven's style "ran counter to what the dominant culture would deem aesthetically pleasing" (Fox 1987, 349). However, style
was not constructed *de novo*; the Coven appropriated style elements from
Victory Village's dominant culture (Levine and Stumpf 1983). Makeup
was not rejected, just makeup used as sexual enticement; religious symbolism was not repudiated, just Christian versions. The Coven practiced
bricolage—the deliberate creation of, not just a Satanic style, but a Satanic
self-concept from available cultural elements. Coven members believed
they became powerful through their connection to the Devil.

> I can do anything when I am with my God. Doesn't matter
> what anybody says. . . . He gives me the power to do any-
> thing. I can be whatever I want to be . . . no one can tell me
> what to do, when to do it. Let them fucking try . . . He [the
> Devil] and I will show them who is the boss. I am.

By acquiring what they considered to be devilish power, Coven members achieved a significant goal—they reversed, in their perception, the
high school's status hierarchies. They were no longer at the bottom
among the "freaks," but were at the very top of the hierarchy—the Satanic chosen few. This new achieved status "worked" for them—they felt
better about themselves.

A challenge from the dominant culture

Identity and self-concept are closely connected with one's social location.
Both non-Satanist adolescents and the Coven used style as a way of proclaiming their social location. The difference is that one group, through
its nonnormative stylistic content, proclaimed its opposition to the dominant cultural values. As their Satanic presentation of self became routinized and recognized by others for what it was, the Coven was sometimes challenged. A local video arcade was the scene of one confrontation.
Five Coven members were in the arcade, surrounding a video game. Two
non-Coven men (members of the junior varsity football team, according
to the t-shirts they were wearing) approached the Coven and began ridi-
culing their Satanic appearance and faith. For a few moments, Coven
members ignored the taunts. Then, after a short whispered conversation,
one of the Coven men turned to the other students and said, "Leave us
the fucking hell alone or else we'll fucking . . ." His voice died out without completing the threat. While he was saying this, he was casually but
deliberately running his finger through the upside down cross hairstyle of
a female member who also was present. One of the challengers immediately took a step backward while fingering the Christian cross on his
necklace. A few moments passed while each side stared intently at the
other, then an employee approached the group and mumbled something
akin to "We don't want trouble here." The football players left the arcade.
Coven members enjoyed this exchange, often describing it and amplify-
ing the encounter. According to members, the story typified how Satan

and therefore the Coven were really the most powerful; after all, it was the *football players* who backed down after just a few moments of confrontation. Several weeks after the incident, Mark, who was present but was not the Coven spokesperson, said to me, "See, they didn't dare fight with us. Those motherfucking big guys were afraid of us. . . . and you ask what Satan has done for me lately?" Interactions such as this one simply reinforced the Coven's conclusion that it, and not the rest of Victory Village, was powerful and in control. In their minds, the status hierarchies had been completely reversed.

However, the stronger and more visible the Satanic style became, the stronger some in the community's concern became. Baron (1989) has noted that, "subcultures, and many of the activities that take place within them, represent 'symbolic violations of the social order' that provoke censure from the dominant culture" (p. 208). The Coven was not able to persuade Victory Village nor the high school to modify their value systems. Indeed, for some members of the community the Coven and its religious critique were considered so disturbing that they demanded social action. Victory Village mobilized to eliminate at least the outward signs of Satanism. There was talk of a high school dress code, which would prohibit visible signs of belonging to the Coven; law enforcement had, for all intents and purposes, closed off the Coven's favorite ritual site, Ghost Bridge, by patrolling it, and the local mall made it clear that, *as a group,* the Coven was not welcome inside—mall security forced them to leave for, according to a security officer, "other customers don't like them."

Despite this community hostility, their Satanic style empowered Coven members. Commitment to the style bonded the group to each other (Fox 1987) and to their new worldview. Thus the development of a Satanic style created a visible collective, though oppositional, identity for the Coven. Both the Coven and members of the community could see the visible accoutrements of Satanic commitment. Coven style norms were expressed through symbolic inversion (Lincoln 1989). It was only by changing themselves—their worldview, their bodies—that the Coven could have any measure of success.

The Coven as oppositional subculture

Culture is transmitted to others through social interaction by parents, teachers, ministers, siblings, and peers. Christian values and norms permeated Victory Village. The statuses of churchgoer, athlete, and cheerleader were valued and rewarded. But the hegemony of this one culture invited a social critic, the Coven. However, the cultural combatants did not have equal social power.

That the Coven existed at all, in the face of so much opposition, at times seemed remarkable: "it is not the accomplishments of such projects [subculture's stated goals] per se that is of paramount importance; rather the very formation of such a group . . . is itself a revolutionary action" (Lincoln 1989, 18). The Coven can illustrate the power of creating new social boundaries. Its continuation was predicted on the intense social bonding that developed within it, and on the ways in which the Satanic worldview gave meaning to members' lives. They transformed a marginal status into an achieved master status, central to their new, oppositional way of life. Lacking the material power to institute social change either in the high school's social structure or in the wider community, the Coven's critique could only operate at the symbolic level.

Analysis of the Coven shows that both the psychiatric and folklore explanations of adolescent Satanism are inadequate. These adolescents were not mentally disturbed, nor were they engaging in major criminal activity. What law-breaking they did—some underage alcohol consumption, minor vandalism of local bridges (spray-painting graffiti), and occasionally driving while intoxicated—are acts many non-Satanist teens also have committed. Nor were they experiencing "just" intergenerational rebellion against their parents. The Coven's critique went far deeper—it questioned the basic values of Victory Village—athleticism, Christianity, heterosexual dyads, and the nature of achievement, beauty, and power.

Yet the "form taken by this resistance [was] somehow *symbolic* or *magical,* in the sense of not being an actual successful solution to whatever is the problem" (Cohen 1980, ix–x). Clothing styles, haircuts, and prayers to Satan did not change the dominant culture of Victory Village. They were not meant to do so. The Coven chose these changes as its way of managing the alienation it found in the social structure of Victory Village and its educational facilities—managing it through confrontation. Oppositional subcultures thrive on conflict; they need it. It is only through confrontation with the dominant culture that their subcultural choices—moral, stylistic, sexual, aesthetic—can be constructed and routinized. Cultural belligerence was the central behavioral tactic of the Coven. It took pleasures in antagonizing Victory Village.

It is through their resistance to community norms that oppositional subcultures gain attention, albeit negative attention. Such opposition allows them to reduce their feelings of alienation or status frustration (Cohen 1955) by creating a new identity that is in contradistinction to their earlier, now rejected, socialization.

Coven members not only did not participate in the male athleticism and female presentation of self. . . , they deliberately ridiculed it.

That a dominant culture reacts to an oppositional subculture's nonnormative behavior by labeling it as deviant or sick and in need of change—something the psychiatric explanation of Satanism has certainly done—may be sociologically understandable. Oppositional groups challenge the entire social system. Institutions of social control must then be utilized to maintain normative order. Thus it was not surprising, in recent years, to see the American therapeutic and religious institutions as well as the mass media mobilized to prevent Satanism from spreading. Given the separation of church and state, these institutions can do little about what Taub and Nelson have called the Satanic Establishment. Such institutions were more able to mobilize themselves around claims about the deviant lifestyles of the alleged Satanic Underground, in particular as it might involve children and adolescents.

However, such claims about underground Satanic criminality, psychosis, substance abuse, and evil need to be investigated by sociologists. The central social actor in these claims—adolescent Satanists who are "out there" worshipping Satan—have been missing from the both the popular and scholarly literature. By listening to their voices it can be shown that, at least for Victory Village's Coven, they were not about murder and mayhem, but social criticism. Their collective goal was not to abuse themselves nor others, but to confront a social system in which they no longer believed. Simplistic categorizations rarely capture the complexities of social life. The Coven was neither part of the Satanic Establishment nor the criminal Satanic Underground. It was an oppositional subculture that chose Satan as the symbol with which to critique its community. In its view, Satan gave members the ability to confront what they found distasteful in their community while giving them a new, important identity. Their theological and cultural inversion of Victory Village's norms was successful for them.

Notes

1. Since 1980, there have been thirteen major talk shows about Satanism (Phil Donahue, Sally Jessy Raphael, Geraldo Rivera, and Oprah Winfrey). For an analysis of how Satanism was constructed on these talk shows, see Lowney (forthcoming).

2. Ellis argued that legend-tripping is mainly done in heterosexual dyadic pairs, not in larger social groupings. He alluded (1991b, 281) to clusters of adolescents who frequent trip sites. "A cluster that specializes in visits to 'haunted' spots may thus be termed an 'occult-oriented folk group,' since members often gather and share knowledge about other aspects of the supernatural and anomalous." But even he does not consider the possibility that adolescent Satanists are an organized social movement.

3. Certainly there are differences between the Coven and the subcultures discussed in these references, the primary one being social class: the Coven consisted almost entirely of middle- and upper-middle-class youths. Nevertheless, there are more similarities than differences.

4. My college's Human Subjects Committee and I communicated in writing about this research several times and met once. This research raised numerous ethical questions. I felt that I might be harming my potential research subjects if I contacted parents who were not aware of their children's activities and asked permission to interview their children about Satanism. Conversely, I felt uneasy contacting parents and obtaining informed consent to ask about "religion in general" when I knew I was interested in only Satanism. The committee for its part, struggled with statutes that did not adequately cover participant observation research. We reached a compromise position: it would be best if I did not interview teenager Satanists unless they had already told their parents about their involvement. I was permitted to obtain birthdate information from potential sources and often followed up with a contact when the person was no longer a minor. For this same reason, I have not collected data at Coven meetings, nor on the grounds of the high schools, because minors often were present. Some data were undoubtedly lost by operating under this compromise, however it provided the only opportunity for the research to continue.

5. Three other times underage members or ex-members showed up to talk with me. For ethical reasons I did not talk to these young adults.

6. For a detailed account of life in another "football town" that has many parallels with Victory Village, see Bissinger (1990). Gaines' (1990) analysis of Bergenfield, New Jersey also noted the linkage between football, social status, and religion.

7. His conversion seems to exemplify the Lofland-Stark model (1965) with two exceptions. Mark was uneasy saying that he was at a "turning point" in his life—he felt that he had always been different—and that high school was no worse, but also no better than previous times in his life. He also had a difficult time sorting out whether extracult attachments had been cut off *before* meeting the group or *after* cult bonds had been formed. On further reflection, Mark could not clearly state that he had *had* any bonds to anyone in the high school prior to joining this group.

8. Following LaVey (1969), the Coven used this term for its ritual meeting time.

9. Again, Ellis's analysis is correct, as far as it goes. Some of these bridges were local legend sites. However, Coven rituals were not connected to these legends.

10. LaVey (1969) has spoken of holding rituals between the four elements of air, water, fire, and earth. Clearly, a bridge meets that criterion.

11. Most law enforcement officers did not feel that the Coven "caused trouble." Their regulation of Coven activities was low-key and mostly focused on underage drinking and driving, spraypainting of graffiti, and bonfires not well doused. Local officers did not "handle" the Coven differently from other teens in the community. This approach was in stark contrast to other jurisdictions present at the Occult Crime workshop I attended. In large measure the Victory Village law enforcement response was led by the sheriff and city police chief, who tried to prevent rumors from spreading.

12. The Coven might have been seen by some outsiders to be a heavy metal subculture. It was only in discussing the religious inversions that it became apparent how important the Satanic theology was in the subculture. It was the latter that set the Coven apart from heavy metal subcultures. See Gross (1990) for a profile of heavy metal subcultures.

13. For instance, this was the first Coven term I encountered during the research. They kept mentioning it, but it took almost a year before such a ritual was explained to me.

References

Alfred, R.H. 1976. The Church of Satan. In *The new religious consciousness*, edited by C.Y. Glock and R.N. Bellah, 180–202. Berkeley: University of California Press.

Bainbridge, W.S. 1978. *Satan's power: A deviant psychotherapy cult*. Berkeley: University of California Press.

Baron, S.W. 1989. Resistance and its consequences: The street culture of punks. *Youth & Society* 21:207–37.

Belitz, J. and A. Schacht. 1992. Satanism as a response to abuse: The dynamics and treatment of Satanic involvement in male youths. *Adolescence* 27:855–72.

Bissinger, H.G. 1990. *Friday night lights: A town, a team, and a dream.* Reading, MA: Addison-Wesley.

Bourget, D., A. Gagnon, and J.M.W. Bradford. 1988. Satanism in a psychiatric adolescent population. *Canadian Journal of Psychiatry* 33:197–202.

Brake, M. 1974. The skinheads: An English working class subculture. *Youth & Society* 6:179–200.

———. 1980. *The sociology of youth culture and youth subcultures.* London: Routledge & Kegan Paul.

Cohen, A. 1955. *Delinquent boys.* Glencoe, IL: Free Press.

Cohen, S. 1980. *Folk devils and moral panics: The creation of the mods and rockers,* 2d ed. New York: St. Martin.

Crouch, B.M., and K.R. Damphousse. 1992. Newspapers and the antisatanism movement: A content analysis. *Sociological Spectrum* 12:1–20.

Ellis, B. 1982–3. Legend-tripping in Ohio: A behavioral survey. *Papers in Comparative Studies* 2:61–73.

———. 1991a. Flying saucers from Hell: Alien abductions and Satanic cult abductions. *Magonia* 40:12–6.

———. 1991b. Legend-trips and Satanism: Adolescents' ostensive traditions as cult activity. In *The Satanism scare,* edited by J.T. Richardson, J. Best, and D.G. Bromley, 279–95. New York: Aldine de Gruyter.

Fine, G.A. 1982. The Manson family: The folklore traditions of a small group. *Journal of the Folklore Institute* 19:47–60.

———. 1987. *With the boys: Little league baseball and preadolescent culture.* Chicago: University of Chicago Press.

Fine, G.A., and S. Kleinman. 1979. Rethinking subculture: An interactionist analysis. *American Journal of Sociology* 85:1–20.

Forsyth, C.J., and M.D. Olivier, 1990. The theoretical framing of a social problem: Some conceptual notes on Satanic cults. *Deviant Behavior* 11:281–92.

Fox, K.J. 1987. Real punks and pretenders: The social organization of a counterculture. *Journal of Contemporary Ethnography* 16:344–70.

Gaines, D. 1990. *Teenage wasteland: Suburbia's dead end kids.* New York: HarperCollins.

Gross, R.L. 1990. Heavy metal music: A new subculture in American society. *Journal of Popular Culture* 24:119–30.

Hebdige, D. 1979. *Subculture: The meaning of style.* London: Methuen & Company.

Hicks, R. 1991a. In pursuit of Satan: The police and the occult. Buffalo, NY: Prometheus.

———. 1991b. The police model of Satanic crime. In *The Satanism scare,* edited by J.T. Richardson, J. Best, and D.G. Bromley, 175–89. New York: Aldine de Gruyter.

Larson, B. 1989. *Satanism, the seduction of America's youth.* Nashville: Thomas Nelson.

LaVey, A.S. 1969. *The Satanic Bible.* New York: Avon.

Levine, H.G., and S.H. Stumpf. 1983. Statements of fear through cultural symbols: Punk rock as reflective subculture. *Youth & Society* 14:417–35.

Lincoln, B. 1989. *Discourse and the construction of society: comparative studies of myth, ritual, and classification.* New York: Oxford.

Lippert, R. 1990. The construction of Satanism as a social problem in Canada. *Canadian Journal of Sociology* 15:417–39.

Lofland, J., and R. Stark. 1965. Becoming a world saver: A theory of conversion to a deviant perspective. *American Sociological Review* 30:863–974.

Lowney, K. Forthcoming. Speak of the devil: Talk shows and the social construction of Satanism. In *Perspectives on Social Problems,* volume 6, edited by J.A. Holstein and G. Miller. Greenwich, CT: JAI.

Moody, E.J. 1974. Magical therapy: An anthropological investigation of contemporary Satanism. In *Religious movements in contemporary America,* edited by I.I. Zaretsky and M.P. Leone, 355–82. Princeton, NJ: Princeton University Press.

Moriarty, A.R., and D.W. Story. 1990. Psychological dynamics of adolescent Satanism. *Journal of Mental Health Counseling* 12:186–98.

The Necronomicon. 1980. Edited with an introduction by Simon. New York: Avon.

Prinsky, L.E., and J.L. Rosenbaum. 1987. Leer-ics or lyrics: Teenage impressions of rock 'n' roll. *Youth & Society* 18:384–97.

Richardson, J.T., J. Best, and D.G. Bromley, eds. 1991a. *The Satanism scare.* New York: Aldine de Gruyter.

Richardson, J.T., J. Best, and D.G. Bromley. 1991b. Satanism as a social problem. In *The Satanism scare,* edited by J.T. Richardson, J. Best, and D.G. Bromley, 3–17. New York: Aldine de Gruyter.

Rudin, Marcia. 1990. Cults and Satanism: Threats to teens. *NAASP Bulletin* 74:46–52.

Speltz, A.M. 1990. Treating adolescent Satanism in art therapy. *The Arts in Psychotherapy* 17:147–55.

Stratford, L. [1987] 1991. *Satan's underground: The extraordinary story of one woman's escape.* Gretna, LA: Pelican.

Steck, G.M., S.A. Anderson, and W.M. Boylin. 1992. Satanism among adolescents: Empirical and clinical considerations. *Adolescence* 27:904–14.

Taub, D., and L.D. Nelson. 1993. Satanism in contemporary America: Establishment or underground. *Sociological Quarterly* 34:523–41.

Tennant-Clark, C.M., J.J. Fritz, and F. Beauvais. 1989. Occult participation: Its impact on adolescent development. *Adolescence* 24:757–72.

Travers, A. 1982. Ritual power in interaction. *Symbolic Interaction* 5:277–86.

Victor, J. 1989. A rumor-panic about a dangerous Satanic cult in western New York. *New York Folklore* 15:23–49.

———. 1991. The dynamics of rumor-panics about Satanic cults. In *The Satanism scare,* edited by J.T Richardson, J. Best, and D.G. Bromley, 221–36. New York: Aldine de Gruyter.

Warnke, Mike. 1972. *The Satan seller.* Plainfield, NJ: Logos International.

Wheeler, B.R., S. Wood, R.J. Hatch. 1988. Assessment and intervention with adolescents involved in Satanism. *Social Work* 33:547–50.

9

Social and Cultural Forces Were Partially Responsible for Satanic Panic

Susan P. Robbins

Susan P. Robbins an associate professor and associate dean for Academic Affairs at the University of Houston Graduate School of Social Work.

The panic over satanic ritual abuse (SRA) is a modern version of the medieval witch hunts. As in the days of the witch hunts, American society was undergoing a significant transformation. Media sensationalism about cults, child pornography, rising crime, economic insecurity, and family instability contributed to the belief in ritual abuse of children. These concerns were enhanced by therapists and counselors who advocated the theory of victimization. These factors combined to make a climate ripe for a societal panic about a satanic conspiracy and satanic ritual abuse.

Beginning in the early 1980s, stories of well-organized satanic cults began to emerge in police reports of horrifying crimes. Not surprisingly, these accounts became increasingly widespread as they also came to be well-publicized by the media. A multigenerational, underground cult network was allegedly orchestrating gruesome satanic rituals that routinely included child sexual abuse, ritualistic torture, mutilation, and human sacrifice (Bromley, 1991; Nathan & Snedeker, 1995). Both media and police reports were based on first-hand accounts of childhood ritual abuse from adults in psychotherapy who claimed that they had "recovered" previously repressed memories, and from young children in day care who allegedly suffered satanic abuse while in the care of Satanist teachers and caretakers (Jenkins, 1992; Jenkins & Maier-Katkin, 1991; Mulhern, 1991; Nathan & Snedeker, 1995; Victor, 1993).

Although these accounts of satanic ritual abuse (SRA) varied to some degree, most shared common themes and were based on anecdotal descriptions of early childhood sexual abuse at the hands of parents or caretakers. Recovered memories of SRA most typically included brainwashing,

From "The Social and Cultural Context of Satanic Ritual Abuse Allegations," by Susan P. Robbins, *Issues in Child Abuse Accusations*, vol. 10, no. 2 (1998). Copyright © 1998 by Institute for Psychological Therapies. Reprinted with permission from the publisher.

being drugged, sexually abused, and being forced to watch or participate in satanic rituals, drinking human blood, and ritual murder. Such early ritual initiation was supposedly preparation for an eventual role as a "breeder" who delivered infants to the satanic cult solely for the purpose of ritual sacrifice. Children in day care who made accusations of SRA against their teachers and caretakers gave accounts of ongoing, and often daily sexual abuse that typically included violent rape, and vaginal and anal mutilation with sharp objects. Such acts allegedly took place during normal day care hours and included the presence of magic rooms, tunnels, clowns, jungle animals, animal mutilation, and flying.

Allegations such as these were often accepted as factual accounts, despite the fantastic nature of the stories and the lack of evidence to support such claims. It was believed, after all, that children would not lie about sexual abuse and that adults could not invent such realistic and consistent memories of horrific abuse.

This article examines the multiple, interrelated, and converging social and cultural forces in American society that gave rise to such SRA allegations and explores the factors that sustained both public and professional belief in widespread ritual abuse. Previous literature in this area has described the influence of specific social factors and trends in the growing therapeutic enterprise (Mulhern, 1991; Nathan & Snedeker, 1995; Pendergrast, 1996; Smith, 1995; Victor, 1993; Wakefield & Underwager, 1994), but none has fully examined the convergence of historical, social, cultural, professional, and ideological forces and their combined influence on the subsequent reporting of and belief in SRA.

The modern satanic cult legend

As Shermer (1997) has pointed out, the recent concern and panic about satanic ritual abuse is a modern version of the medieval witch crazes. In such crazes, the intermeshing of psychological and social conditions become coupled with a feedback loop that feeds on people's fears and drives legends and rumor panics in such a way that they come to have a life of their own. Although a variety of commonalities between historical witch crazes and modern SRA accusations have been noted in the literature, some of the most salient similarities include: 1) the prevalence of allegations of sex or sexual abuse; 2) mere accusations become equated with factual guilt; 3) the denial of guilt is seen as proof of guilt; 4) single claims of victimization lead to an outbreak of similar claims; and 5) as the accused begin to fight back, the pendulum begins to swing the other way as the accusers sometimes become the accused, and the falsity of the accusations is demonstrated by skeptics (Shermer, 1997).

The role of various stakeholders, discussed in more detail below, plays an important part in the escalation of rumor panics and, as Victor (1993) has demonstrated, the modern SRA legend is not dissimilar to other rumor-driven panics that have been promulgated and further legitimized by self-proclaimed authority figures. Very significantly, legends of this sort have great mass appeal because they provide simple explanations for disturbing phenomena in society.

Central to the modern SRA legend are fears about evil acts perpetuated on children that include kidnapping, murder, molestation, child slavery, child pornography, and child sacrifice for satanic purposes (Richardson, Best & Bromley, 1991). While such fears may be rooted, in part, in real dangers, they have been found to be widely over-exaggerated and exacerbated by questionable public statistics that warn of a host of dangers to children. Underlying such fears is a primary concern regarding the sexual abuse of children.

Despite the fact that sexual abuse of children is a very real and tragic social problem, public concern about child abuse and CSA [child sexual abuse] was not mobilized until these were publicly defined as a problem that cut across social class boundaries (see Costin, Karger & Stoesz, 1996; Hacking, 1995; Pelton, 1981). Although the data have consistently and clearly indicated that violence, child abuse, and CSA are strongly over-represented among the poor, the myth of classlessness and the subsequent acceptance of child abuse as a middle-class problem was a key factor in the spread of our current concept of CSA. In addition to separating the problem of abuse from the less appealing issue of violence associated with persistent poverty, the new mythology of abuse became extremely profitable for the growing industries of psychotherapy and law. It also increased the likelihood that legislation would be passed and funded to provide services that were not linked directly to conditions of poverty (Costin, Karger & Stoesz, 1996; Pelton, 1981).

It is within this social and cultural context that allegations of CSA and SRA in day care settings first arose in the early 1980s. Although satanic cult rumors predated this by more than a decade, the first ritual child abuse allegations and arrests occurred in 1983 in the famous McMartin Preschool case (Victor, 1993). According to Nathan (1991), by mid-1984 reports of ritual child abuse skyrocketed and, by 1987, over 100 such cases had been validated by child protection agencies and police, despite the total lack of admissible evidence in many cases. In response to such allegations, criminal evidence statutes were reformed to make it easier to prosecute such cases and a new cadre of police, mental health, and child welfare "specialists" claiming expertise in SRA developed new methods to elicit SRA affirmations and discourage denial and recantation. As these new and questionable methods were taught to other professionals through a series of training seminars and specialty conferences, the epidemic of accusations of ritual abuse in day care settings began to grow as well.

The demonization of cults

Concern about satanic cults and satanic crime, however, was predated by a growing widespread alarm about religious cults since they first emerged in the United States in the late 1960s and early 1970s. The media gave special attention to a variety of relatively new, small, non-traditional religious groups that proliferated during this time period (Beckford, 1985; Robbins, 1992). The popular use of the term "cult" generally carries with it extremely pejorative connotations, and such groups are viewed as essentially deviant and controversial due to their unconventional beliefs and lifestyles, and often totalistic separatism from mainstream society (Beckford, 1985; Robbins, 1992; Shupe & Bromley, 1991).

By the mid 1970s, stereotypes of cults as being "dangerous," "extreme," and "destructive" began to emerge, and anti-cult sentiment was further solidified with the 1978 mass suicide/murder of the followers of charismatic leader Reverend Jim Jones in Jonestown, Guyana. From this point on cults were seen as groups that were brainwashed into submission and labeled as being authoritarian, totalistic, dangerous, destructive, fanatic, and violent (Victor, 1993). Despite a growing body of empirical research that questioned the validity of this stereotype and demonstrated that most new religious groups are, instead, characterized by an impressive diversity, these ideas became central to the negative conception of satanic cults as well (Beckford, 1985; Robbins, 1995a, 1997; Victor, 1993).

Satanic cults and the new "crime wave"

By the late 1980s societal concern turned to reports of a new "crime wave" that connected violent crimes to occult practices and satanic worship (see Larson, 1989; Raschke, 1990; Schwarz & Empey, 1988). Satanism became linked to the use of ritualistic magic and animal sacrifice in religions with African and Hispanic origins such as Voodoo, Santeria, and Brujeria (Kahaner, 1988). Growing reports of cult-related child sexual abuse (CSA) and recovered memories of SRA added fuel to the increasing hysteria about coercion and brainwashing within satanic cults and previously unrevealed and unthinkable forms of horrific cultic crime.

Despite the growing hysteria, studies have consistently shown that there is no reliable empirical evidence to support allegations of widespread, organized, multigenerational satanic crime (Blimling, 1991; Bromley, 1991; Jenkins, 1992; Lyons, 1988; Melton, 1986a; Richardson et al., 1991; Victor, 1993). Numerous and extensive police and FBI investigations have concluded that there is no definitive physical evidence that such cultic crime exists (see Bromley, 1991; Lanning, 1989a, 1989b; Lyons, 1988; Victor, 1993).

Contemporary Satanism, on the other hand, does exist, and is manifested primarily in two forms: 1) open satanic groups and churches that pose no public threat; and 2) small ephemeral groups of self-proclaimed Satanists, composed primarily of teenagers and young adults (Melton, 1986b). In addition to these groups, individuals who have no group affiliations may be involved in their own version of satanic worship. Both individuals and groups of self-proclaimed satanists are frequently involved in violent crimes such as murder and rape, as well as crimes involving drug trafficking. The causal link between organized satanic worship and the crimes committed by these individuals is, at best, tenuous (see Lyons, 1988; Ofshe, 1986; Victor, 1993).

The news media have played an important role in the general public's perception of and belief in satanic cults and cultic crime.

Although there is no evidence to support the claims of widespread satanic crime, proponents of satanic conspiracy theory continue to pose an argument that is virtually irrefutable (Bromley, 1991). The lack of evidence is cited as "proof" of the successful clandestine operation of the cult. Thus, according to Victor (1993), "sensational claims" of cult survivors have come to be transformed into irrefutable "truths."

Anti-cult organizations

The rise of new religious cults in the 1960s and 70s led to the formation of anti-cult groups that were initially composed of parents who were concerned about losing their children to destructive cults (Robbins, 1992; Shupe & Bromley, 1991; Victor, 1993). By the 1980s, anti-cult groups achieved greater organizational stability, and were able to draw media attention to their cause. Central to their allegations was the idea that cult members were victims of brainwashing that was achieved through the use of drugs, hypnotism, and other forms of coercive mind control (Shupe & Bromley, 1991). As the anti-cult movement became more sophisticated, they forged an alliance with sympathetic social workers, psychologists, psychiatrists, social scientists, lawyers, and police. Professional newsletters, journals, monographs, and seminars on destructive cultism quickly proliferated and gave greater credibility to the idea that cult members were victims of mind control.

As reports of satanic crime and SRA began to surface in the 1980s, parallel coalitions emerged to confront what they believed to be the new and growing threat of satanic cults. Similar to the dissemination of earlier allegations of cultic mind control, claims of a satanic conspiracy, CSA, ritualistic abuse, and kidnapping were quickly spread through conferences and literature for police and mental health counselors, through fundamentalist articles, books, and radio programs. Eventually, sensationalistic stories of SRA made their way into the mainstream media (Bromley, 1991; Crouch & Damphouse, 1991; Jenkins, 1992; Victor, 1993).

The influence of the media

The news media have played an important role in the general public's perception of and belief in satanic cults and cultic crime. The tendency of the media to report sensationalistic stories about SRA and cultic crime greatly contributed to a widespread belief in the reality of ritualistic abuse (Richardson et al., 1991; Victor, 1993).

Newspaper and magazine reports on satanic cults relied heavily on officials and cult "experts" who portray all forms of Satanism and cult membership as dangerous and destructive. During the 1980s, terrifying accounts of SRA and cult victimization were commonly featured on national television talk-show programs such as "Geraldo" and "Oprah Winfrey" (Richardson et al., 1991; Rowe & Cavender, 1991; Victor, 1993). Divergent views, though aired, were frequently overshadowed by horrific stories of a satanic conspiracy, mind control, ritualistic torture and sexual abuse. Not surprisingly, divergent views were often seen by the general public as less credible than firsthand accounts of abuse and torture. Quite simply, it was incomprehensible to think that anyone would lie about such events.

Common portrayals of Satanism by anti-cult groups and alleged SRA survivors included diverse practices such as kidnapping, ritual sexual abuse, sacrifice of children, cannibalism, blood drinking, and animal mutilations. Perhaps most significantly, when unfounded allegations about such crimes and practices were proven to be untrue, they received sparse media attention. Thus, uncritical and sensationalized reporting have helped shape, support, and perpetuate the public's belief in SRA and cultic crime (Robbins, 1995a, 1997).

The recovered memory movement

Because many of the reports of SRA were based on memories recovered in the course of therapy, one of the significant factors in the spread of SRA stories was the rediscovery and embracing of Freudian theory by professionals and paraprofessionals in the field of mental health (Robbins, 1995b). Freud originally believed that repressed memories of early childhood seduction were responsible for much of the psychopathology that he encountered in his psychoanalytic practice. He later revised his position and, although he continued to believe in his patients' conscious and spontaneously reported memories of abuse, he came to doubt the veracity of unconscious memories of early infantile seduction, which he concluded, "were only phantasies which my patients had made up or which I myself had perhaps forced on them" (Freud cited in Demause, 1991, p. 126). Thus, in accordance with Freud's revision of his early theory, psychoanalysts and therapists trained in neo-Freudian thought were taught that patient reports of seduction and sexual abuse were incestuous wishes rather than memories of actual events (Masson, 1990).

By the mid-to-late 1970s, feminist researchers and therapists began to document the reality of CSA and brought it to the forefront as a public issue. Recognition of the reality of CSA was long overdue because most mental health professionals ignored, minimized, or avoided the topic of sexual abuse for a variety of social, cultural, and professional reasons (Craine, Henson, Colliver, & MacLean, 1988; Jacobson, Koehler, & Jones-Brown, 1987; Nathan & Snedeker, 1995; Post et al., 1980; Rose, Peabody, & Stratigeas, 1991). Given the prevalence of abuse found in clinical populations, the failure to inquire about or respond to reports of sexual abuse was, indeed, a serious omission (Robbins, 1995b).

As neo-Freudian thought began to be displaced by biological psychiatry and family systems approaches (among others) in the early-to-mid 1980s, influential psychoanalysts began to revive Freud's early theory of childhood seduction. Expanding on Freud's early theory and British psychoanalyst Fairbairn's object-relations revision of repressed sexual trauma (1952), Swiss psychoanalyst, Alice Miller (1981, 1983, 1984) was among the first to popularize what has now become the common conception of repressed childhood trauma at the hands of one's parents. Further building on the tragic reality of incest and the revived concept of repressed sexual trauma, psychiatrist Judith Herman's book *Father-Daughter Incest* provided early impetus for the formation of incest survivor therapy groups in the Boston area (Webster, 1995). Perhaps even more influential was the work of psychoanalyst Jeffrey Masson, the former projects director of the Freud archives. In his now famous book *The Assault on Truth: Freud's Suppression of the Seduction Theory* (1984), Masson proposed that for personal, political, and professionally expedient reasons, Freud abandoned his theory about the importance of incest in the development of hysteria.

As Pendergrast (1996, p. 423) noted, Masson's work has served as "one of the cornerstones of the Incest Survivor movement." The revival of Freudian seduction theory led the way for what would soon become a largely uncritical acceptance of uncorroborated accounts of repressed memories of repeated sexual abuse and recovered memories of SRA.

Addiction, denial, and the self-help movement

The expansion of recovered memory ideology was aided by a new and growing social and cultural phenomenon that emerged in the 1980s: the growth in the size and scope of self-help groups based on the twelve step model of Alcoholics Anonymous (AA). The escalation of "zero tolerance" in the War on Drugs and the concomitant push for widespread identification and treatment of substance abuse was eagerly embraced by the media. Estimated and fabricated figures that warned of the growing prevalence of alcoholism and illegal drug use became commonplace (Baum, 1996; Peele, 1989). The resulting growth in the substance abuse treatment industry was aided by media campaigns that included testimonials by well-known people such as Kitty Dukakis, Betty Ford, and Elizabeth Taylor, whose stories were aimed at convincing people to get help for their addictions. Thus, as Peele (1989) has pointed out, addiction not only became destigmatized, but addicts were turned into role models. As drug treatment programs came to rely heavily on AA ideology and group treatment methods, the AA credo of twelve step recovery became a national dogma (Peele, 1989).

Ironically, even though AA had enjoyed some degree of popularity since its inception in the 1930s, the ideology of self-help recovery in the 1980s began to shift some of the ideas that were central to AA. Instead of people seeking help because they knew that they were having problems with alcohol, alcoholics were now seen as being in denial about their illness (Peele, 1989).

As the idea of denial became popularized, the ever-expanding concept of "addiction" and twelve step recovery began to spread to a wide variety of other behaviors such as eating, gambling, sex, love, and relationships. Groups like Al-Anon and Alateen that were initially set up to provide support and guidance for non-alcoholic family members, now began to portray wives, husbands, parents, and children of the alcoholic as themselves having a disease. Alcoholism and drug addiction were no longer seen as an illness of the individual alcoholic or addict, but of the entire family system. Denial was defined as "part of the disease for both the alcoholic and his family" (Woititz, 1976). With denial at the core, the newly popularized concepts of "co-dependency" and the "dysfunctional family" gave rise to a burgeoning self-help industry in which all of life's problems were defined as a previously undiagnosed disease, rooted in childhood family dysfunction, over which the sufferers had little, if any, control.

Pop psychology, feminist theory, and survivor ideology

The addiction self-help movement provided fertile ground for the expansion of theories and ideology to support the growing view of families, and society as a whole, as being diseased and dysfunctional. Rather than examining some of the very real and social and economic stressors that accompanied the quickly changing and unstable job market, fluctuating economy, profound changes in family structure, changing social roles, and the increasing demands on women, many of whom now found it necessary to join the labor market as well as be responsible for child care, the disease model turned our attention inward and backward. Newly self-appointed "experts" in addiction and dysfunction turned to the prototypical Freudian model of individual pathological functioning based on alleged parenting deficiencies in early childhood (Kaminer, 1993; Pendergrast, 1996; Smith, 1995). Popularized versions of Freudian-based object-relations theory emerged as one of the primary theoretical explanations of adult dysfunction (see Smith, 1995; Wood, 1987).

Although early American feminists criticized Freudian theory for its distinctively anti-female assumptions, later feminist thought embraced a revised form of psychoanalytic theory that accepted many of Freud's fundamental assumptions about the nature of the unconscious and the importance of early childhood experiences in the formation of adult personality (see Chodorow, 1978). While rejecting the idea of female inferiority that was pivotal to Freud's work, both psychoanalytic feminism and an emerging body of radical feminist writing portrayed male domination (i.e. the patriarchy) as the root of women's oppression and the primary cause of psychological disorders. Violence against women (physical, sexual, and psychological) was seen as a primary force through which women were denied control over their lives and choices.

The recovered memory movement readily embraced the idea of male violence, particularly that of repressed CSA at the hands of fathers, step-fathers, and other male authority figures. Women (overwhelmingly white and middle class) who sought counseling for alcohol and drug problems, depression, eating disorders, and a variety of other conditions were told by their therapists that they were abuse victims because they showed the "symptoms" of CSA, despite the fact that most had no conscious memories of such childhood violence. Many were encouraged to "abreact," or recover and relive the repressed memories, and to join ongoing incest survivor self-help groups to aid in their "recovery."

More recently, a newer "third wave" of feminism has produced scathing critiques about feminist theory and practice that is rooted in the concept of victimization (see Kaminer, 1995; Robbins, Chatterjee, & Canda, 1998). Requiring women to assume the role of the "victim," a person who is perpetually in recovery, has been criticized for being disempowering as well as being a suppression of women's rights to sexual, psychological, and economic freedom. Nonetheless, "victim feminism," as it has been dubbed, was an integral part of the recovery culture that emerged in the 1980s.

The recovery culture and the rise of SRA

In the context of a variety of self-help recovery groups, women came to adopt the view of themselves as co-dependent, dysfunctional and "diseased," and they came to accept their therapist's and recovery group's definitions of the cause and nature of their problems.

Among the burgeoning self-help recovery literature on addictions, codependency, sexual abuse, and family dysfunction, the publication of a pivotal book, *The Courage to Heal: A Guide for Women Survivors of Child Sexual Abuse*, advanced the purely ideological position that "if you think you were abused, and your life shows the symptoms, then you were" (Bass & Davis, 1994.) Written by two women with no formal training in psychology or counseling, this book became the veritable bible of the sexual abuse survivor movement. With victimization now elevated to an even higher and more desirable status, women were told, and many came to believe, that they could not trust themselves, their self-knowledge, or their actual memories. Ironically, this new therapeutic ideology, allegedly rooted in feminist thought and concern for women, actually replicated the oppressive patriarchal model of therapy in which the patient's self-knowledge was inferior to the therapist's expertise.

One of the significant factors in the spread of [satanic ritual abuse] stories was the rediscovery and embracing of Freudian theory [of recovered memory].

Newly "recovered" memories of CSA were sometimes accompanied by even more horrific accounts of childhood abuse that included torture, abuse, and murder in satanic cults. Although some of these stories first surfaced in the early 1980s (Nathan, 1991), they became quickly fueled and spread by the popular media, and an uncritical belief on the part of a small cohort of therapists that their patients' accounts reflected real memories of cult abuse. In this context, SRA survivor stories became a primary focus of therapy. New and often barbaric techniques to invoke abreaction were taught at professional seminars and were justified by the idea that SRA survivors suffered Multiple Personality Disorder (later renamed Dissociative Identity Disorder) that was reinforced by sadistic satanic cult brainwashing.

As SRA and MPD became inextricably linked with one another, stories of satanic abuse gained credibility through their association with a psychiatric diagnosis. Through its inclusion in the primary manual used to diagnose psychiatric disorders, the aura of medical acceptance validated the treatment of satanic possession and abuse, despite the fact that there was no verifiable evidence that any such abuse had occurred. Skeptics were always critical of this diagnosis and were quick to label MPD an "iatrogenic" disorder, a disorder that is actually caused by the treatment itself. Although SRA claims are now being examined with a more critical eye by the media and most therapists, the diagnosis of MPD/DID continues to be linked to dissociated childhood trauma.

Many therapists are now approaching such cases more cautiously, however, due to the fact that a large number of people have now recanted their SRA "memories," questioned their diagnosis of MPD/DID, and some have won very high profile lawsuits against their therapists for implanting memories of SRA and CSA that never occurred. In addition, professional organizations that regulate mental health counseling have now issued statements or guidelines warning about the use of hypnosis and other therapeutic methods aimed at the recovery of repressed memories (Pendergrast, 1996).

The numerous social and cultural forces that gave rise to the widespread belief in SRA coalesced at a time in which American society was undergoing significant transformation. New societal fears about cults, child pornography, rising crime, family instability, and a growing concern for children's safety, all contributed to the belief in the ritual abuse of children. Fueled by media sensationalism, these apprehensions and concerns became further enhanced by a growing self-help movement and counseling industry based on defining life's problems in terms of addictions and one's status as a victim. This was then coupled with the renewed ideological belief that present day problems stem from early childhood trauma and family dysfunction. This paved the way, in part, for the rise of an increasingly profitable therapeutic enterprise built on people's fears and dissatisfaction.

Although many of these forces were interactive and intricately built upon one another, they must also be placed within the larger social context of the day in which real and unsettling changes in the industrial economy were accompanied by economic insecurity, changing family forms, and increasing anxiety about family stability and sex roles. It is the confluence of these multiple factors that made the climate ripe for a rumor panic about a satanic conspiracy that led otherwise reasonable people to believe in fantastic and unfounded accounts of satanic ritual abuse.

References

Bass, E., & Davis, L. (1994). *The Courage to Heal: A Guide for Women Survivors of Sexual Abuse*. New York: Harper & Row.

Baum, D. (1996). *Smoke and Mirrors*. Boston: Little, Brown.

Beckford, J.A. (1985). *Cult Controversies: The Societal Response to New Religious Movements*. New York: Tavistock.

Blimling, G.S. (1991, March). Youth and the occult. Paper presented at the annual program meeting of the Council on Social Work Education, New Orleans.

Bromley, D.G. (1991). Satanism: The new cult scare. In J.T. Richardson, J. Best, & D.G. Bromley (Eds.), *The Satanism Scare* (pp. 49–72). Hawthorne, NY: Aldine De Gruyter.

Chodorow, N. (1978). The Reproduction of Mothering: Psychoanalysis and the Sociology of Gender. Berkeley: University of California Press.

Costin, L.B., Karger, H.J., & Stoesz, D. (1996). *The Politics of Child Abuse in America*. New York: Oxford University Press.

Crain, L.S., Henson, C.E., Colliver, J.A. & MacLean, D.G. (1988). Prevalence of a history of sexual abuse among female psychiatric patients in a state hospital system. *Hospital and Community Psychiatry*, 39, 300–304.

Crouch, B.E. & Damphouse, K. (1991). Law enforcement and the Satanism-crime connection: A survey of "cult cops". In J.T. Richardson, J. Best, & D.G. Bromley (Eds.), *The Satanism Scare* (pp. 191–217). Hawthorne, NY: Aldine De Gruyter.

Demause, L. (1991). The universality of incest. Journal of Psychohistory, 19, 123–164.

Fairbairn, W.R.D. (1952). *Psychoanalytic Studies of the Personality*. New York: Basic Books.

Hacking, I. (1995). *Rewriting the Soul: Multiple Personality and the Sciences of Memory*. Princeton, NJ: Princeton University Press.

Herman, J.L. (1981). *Father-Daughter Incest.* Cambridge, MA: Harvard University Press.

Jacobson, A., Koehler, J., & Jones-Brown, C. (1987). The failure of routine assessment to detect histories of assault experienced by psychiatric patients. *Hospital and Community Psychiatry*, 38, 386–389.

Jenkins, P. (1992). Intimate Enemies. Hawthorne, NY: Aldine De Gruyter.

Jenkins, P., & Maier-Katkin, D. (1991). Occult survivors: The making of a myth. In J.T. Richardson, J. Best, & D.G. Bromley (Eds.), *The Satanism Scare* (pp. 127–144). Hawthorne, NY: Aldine De Gruyter.

Kahaner, L. (1988). *Cults That Kill.* New York: Warner.

Kaminer, W. (1993). *I'm Dysfunctional, You're Dysfunctional.* New York: Vintage Books.

Kaminer, W. (1995) *It's All the Rage: Crime and Culture.* Reading, MA: Addison-Wesley Pub.

Lanning, K.V. (1989a). Satanic, occult, and ritualistic crime; A law enforcement perspective. *The Police Chief*, LVI, 62–63.

Lanning, K.V. (1989b). *Child sex rings: A behavioral analysis.* Washington, DC: National Center for Missing and Exploited Children.

Larson, B. (1989). *Satanism: The Seduction of America's Youth.* Nashville: Thomas Nelson Press.

Lyons, A. (1988). *Satan Wants You: The Cult of Devil Worship in America.* New York: Mysterious Press.

Masson, J.M. (1984). *The Assault on Truth: Freud's Suppression of the Seduction Theory.* New York: HarperCollins.

Masson, J.M. (1990) *Final Analysis: The Making and Unmaking of a Psychoanalyst.* Reading, MA: Addison-Wesley Pub.

Melton, J.G. (1986a). *Encyclopedic Handbook of Cults in America.* New York: Garland.

Melton, J.G. (1986b, March). Evidences of Satan in contemporary America: A survey. Paper presented at the Pacific Division of the American Philosophical Association, Los Angeles.

Miller, A. (1981). *Prisoners of childhood.* New York: Basic Books.

Miller, A. (1983). *For Your Own Good: Hidden Cruelty in Child-Rearing and the Roots of Violence.* New York: Farrar, Straus & Giroux.

Miller, A. (1984). *Thou Shalt Not Be Aware: Society's Betrayal of the Child.* New York: Farrar, Straus & Giroux.

Mulhern, S. (1991). Satanism and psychotherapy. In J.T. Richardson, J. Best, & D.G. Bromley (Eds.), *The Satanism Scare* (pp. 145–172). Hawthorne, NY: Aldine De Gruyter.

Nathan, D. (1991). Satanism and child molestation: Constructing the ritual abuse scare. In J.T. Richardson, J. Best, & D.G. Bromley (Eds.), *The Satanism Scare* (pp. 75–94). Hawthorne, NY: Aldine De Gruyter.

Nathan D., and Snedeker, M. (1995). *Satan's Silence.* NY: Basic Books.

Ofshe, R. (1986, September 2). Satanism: Overtones in other slayings. *Los Angeles Times*, pp. 1–2.

Peele, S. (1989). *Diseasing of America: Addiction Treatment Out of Control.* Boston: Houghton Mifflin.

Pelton, L.H. (1981). The myth of classlessness. In L.H. Pelton, (Ed.), *The Social Context of Child Abuse and Neglect.* New York: Human Sciences Press.

Pendergrast, M. (1996). *Victims of Memory* (2nd Ed.). Hinesberg, VT: Upper Access Books.

Post, R.D., Willett, A.B., Franks, R.D., House, R.M., & Weissberg, M.P. (1980). A preliminary report on the prevalence of domestic violence among psychiatric inpatients. *American Journal of Psychiatry*, 137, 974–975.

Raschke, C.A. (1990). *Painted Black: From Drug Killings to Heavy Metal—How Satanism Is Besieging Our Culture and Our Communities*. San Francisco: Harper & Row.

Richardson, J.T., Best, J., & Bromley, D.G. (Eds.). (1991). *The Satanism Scare*. Hawthorne, NY: Aldine De Gruyter.

Robbins, S.P. (1995a). *Cults*. Encyclopedia of Social Work, 19th Edition, Washington, DC: NASW Press, 667–677.

Robbins, S.P. (1995b). Wading through the muddy waters of recovered memories. *Families in Society*, 76(8), 478–489.

Robbins, S.P. (1997). *Cults* (update). Encyclopedia of Social Work, 19th Edition on CD ROM. Washington, DC: National Association of Social Workers Press.

Robbins, S.P., Chatterjee, P., & Canda, E.R. (1998). *Contemporary Human Behavior Theory: A Critical Perspective for Social Work*. Boston: Allyn and Bacon.

Robbins, T. (1992). *Cults, Converts and Charisma*. Newbury Park, CA: Sage.

Rose, S.M., Peabody, C.G., & Stratigeas, B. (1991). Responding to hidden abuse: A role for social work in reforming mental health systems. *Social Work*, 36(5), 408–413.

Rowe, L., & Cavender, G. (1991). Caldrons bubble, Satan's trouble, but witches are okay: Media constructions of Satanism and witchcraft. In J.T. Richardson, J. Best, and D.G. Bromley (Eds.), *The Satanism Scare* (pp. 263–275). Hawthorne, NY: Aldine De Gruyter.

Schwarz, T., & Empey, D. (1988). *Satanism: Is Your Family Safe?* Grand Rapids, MI: Zondervan.

Shermer, M. (1997). *Why People Believe Weird Things: Pseudoscience, Superstition, and Other Confusions of Our Time*. New York: W.H. Freeman and Co.

Shupe, A., & Bromley, D.G. (1991, August). The modern American anti-cult movement: A twenty year retrospective. Paper presented at the annual meeting of the Association for the Sociology of Religion, Cincinnati.

Smith, S. (1995). *Survivor Psychology: The Dark Side of a Mental Health Mission*. Boca Raton, FL: SIRS Press.

Victor, J.S. (1993). *Satanic Panic: The Creation of a Contemporary Legend*. Chicago: Open Court Publishing.

Wakefield, H., & Underwager, R. (1994). *Return of the Furies: An Investigation Into Recovered Memory Therapy*. Chicago: Open Court Publishing.

Webster, R. (1995). *Why Freud Was Wrong: Sin, Science and Psychoanalysis*. New York: Basic Books.

Woititz, J.G. (1976). A study of self-esteem in the children of alcoholics. Ph.D. Dissertation, Rutgers University.

Wood, B.L. (1987). *Children of Alcoholism: The Struggle For Self and Intimacy in Adult Life*. New York: New York University Press.

Organizations to Contact

The editors have compiled the following list of organizations concerned with the issues debated in this book. The descriptions are derived from materials provided by the organizations. All have publications or information available for interested readers. The list was compiled on the date of publication of the present volume; the information provided here may change. Be aware that many organizations take several weeks or longer to respond to inquiries, so allow as much time as possible.

American Family Foundation (AFF)
PO Box 413005, Naples, FL 34101-3005
(941) 514-3081 • fax: (941) 514-3451
e-mail: infoserv@affcultinfoserve.com • website: www.csj.org

AFF is a secular research organization that studies psychological manipulation and cults. Its mission is to educate the public and help those who have been adversely affected by participation in a cult. It publishes the research journal *Cultic Studies Journal*, the newsletter *Cult Observer*, and the study guide "Satanism and Occult-Ritual Activity: Questions and Answers."

Christian Research Institute (CRI)
PO Box 7000, Rancho Santa Margarita, CA 92688-7000
56051 Airways PO, Calgary, Alberta T2E 85K
(949) 858-6100 • fax: (949) 858-6111 Canada: (800) 665-5851

The Christian Research Institute seeks to encourage orthodox, biblical Christianity. CRI disseminates information on cults, the occult, and other religious movements whose teachings and practices are inconsistent with the institute's biblical views. The institute publishes the *Christian Research Journal*, the *Christian Research Newsletter*, and the articles "What About Halloween?" and "The Hard Facts About Satanic Ritual Abuse," among others.

Church of Satan (CoS)
P.O. Box 390009, San Diego, CA 92149-0009
e-mail: nadramia@panix.com • website: www.churchofsatan.com

The Church of Satan was founded on April 30, 1966, by Anton Szandor LaVey and is the first religion devoted to Satan. The church is openly dedicated to the acceptance of humankind's true nature—that of a carnal beast, living in a cosmos which is permeated and motivated by the Dark Force called Satan. Satanists believe they are their own gods. Its website offers published interviews with LaVey and articles explaining the theory and practice of Satanism and satanic thought.

Cult Awareness Network (CAN)
1680 N. Vine, Suite 415, Los Angeles, CA 90028
(800) 556-3055 • fax: (323) 468-0562
e-mail: can@cultawarenessnetwork.org
website: www.cultawarenessnetwork.org

CAN's primary goal is to promote religious freedom and the protection of religious and civil rights. CAN gathers information about diverse groups and religions, maintains an extensive reference database, and sponsors conferences open to the public. The network also staffs a national hotline for individuals who are concerned that their friends or relatives may be involved with a questionable religious group. CAN publishes a newsletter periodically as well as a variety of brochures and booklets on religious conversions, belief systems, life styles, and related issues.

False Memory Syndrome Foundation (FMSF)
1955 Locust St., Philadelphia, PA 19103-5766
(215) 940-1040 • fax: (215) 940-1042
website: www.fmsfonline.com

The FMSF documents and studies cases of adult children who suddenly have recovered repressed memories of childhood abuse. The foundation has a separate database that provides information, copies of journal articles, and reports that are skeptical of claims of satanic ritual abuse and repressed memories. It also publishes the bimonthly *FMS Foundation Newsletter.*

First Church of Satan (FCoS)
PMB 172, 203 Washington St., Salem, MA 01970
website: www.churchofsatan.org

The First Church of Satan is an offshoot of the original Church of Satan. According to the FCoS, there is a race of beings, known as daemons, that is more developed, spiritually and physically, than humankind. The church also believes that daemons are the progenitors of humans, that humans are inherently divine, and that humans create God in their own image. The First Church of Satan's website offers many articles on its beliefs and philosophy, including "The Complete Sermons of Lucifer," "The Satanic Trinity," and "Children and the Left-Hand Path."

Ontario Consultants on Religious Tolerance
PO Box 514, Wellesley Island, NY 13640-0514
Box 27026, Frontenac PO, Kingston ON Canada K7M 8W5
fax: (613) 547-9015
website: www.religioustolerance.org

The Ontario Consultants on Religious Tolerance is composed of a small group of volunteers who provide accurate information about minority religions (including Satanism), religious fraud, hatred, and current religious topics. It hopes its efforts to counter misinformation spread by others will lead to understanding and tolerance and decrease bigotry. The organization presents, compares, and contrasts all sides of each issue in its publications, such as "Does Satanic Ritual Abuse Exist?" and "Satanism: Religious Satanism, Gothic Satanism, Satanic Dabbling, Etc."

Spiritual Counterfeits Project (SCP)
PO Box 4308, Berkeley, CA 94704
(510) 540-0300 • (510) 540-1107
e-mail: access@scp-inc.org • website: www.scp-inc.org

SCP is a Christian ministry that monitors spiritual trends, including cults, the occult, Eastern religions, and the New Age movement. The organization maintains an extensive library with files on cults and new religious movements and offers films, tapes, leaflets, outreach services, and counseling to the public. Its publications include the *SCP Newsletter* and the *SCP Journal*, as well as a variety of books and educational materials.

Temple of Set
PO Box 470307, San Francisco, CA 94147
e-mail: ED@xeper.org • website: www.xeper.org

The Temple of Set broke off from the Church of Satan during the 1970s. Believers worship the Egyptian god Set, whose priesthood can be traced to predynastic times. Set is the oldest known form of the Prince of Darkness. The temple is designed as a tool for personal empowerment, self-cultivation, and above all, to honor and enshrine consciousness. The Temple of Set's website offers many articles on its philosophy and beliefs, such as "Why Should I Join the Temple of Set?" "Setian Philosophy," and "Xeper: The Eternal Word of Set."

Watchman Fellowship
PO Box 13340, Arlington, Texas 76094
(817) 277-0023 • fax: (817) 277-8098
website: www.watchman.org

The Watchman Fellowship specializes in the study of new religious movements, including cults, the occult, and the New Age movement. The organization researches claims of questionable cult practices and provides counseling for former cult members. It offers several articles, videotapes, and books on Satanism, and publishes the *Watchman Expositor* magazine.

Wellspring Retreat and Resource Center
PO Box 67, Albany, OH 45710
(740) 698-6277 • fax: (740) 698-2053
website: www.wellspringretreat.org

Wellspring provides treatment and counseling for victims of cultic or religious abuse or mind control. The center researches and archives information on the various groups, cults, and cult phenomenon. It offers numerous books and articles about cults and victims of cults, and publishes the *Wellspring Journal*.

Bibliography

Books

Gavin Baddeley — *Lucifer Rising: A Book of Sin, Devil Worship and Rock 'n' Roll*. Medford, NJ: Plexus, 1999.

David V. Barrett — *Sects, "Cults," and Alternative Religions: A World Survey and Sourcebook*. London: Blandford, 1998.

J.H. Brennan — *Magick for Beginners: The Power to Change Your World*. St. Paul, MN: Llewellyn, 1999.

Raymond Buckland — *Practical Candleburning Rituals*. St. Paul, MN: Llewellyn, 1999.

Nigel Cawthorne — *Satanic Murder: Chilling True Stories of Sacrificial Slaughter*. London: True Crime, 1995.

Bill Ellis — *Raising the Devil: Satanism, New Religions, and the Media*. Lexington: University Press of Kentucky, 2000.

Marc Galanter — *Cults: Faith, Healing, and Coercion*. 2nd ed. New York: Oxford University Press, 1999.

J.S. LaFontaine — *Speak of the Devil: Tales of Satanic Abuse in Contemporary England*. Cambridge UK: Cambridge University Press, 1998.

Bob Larson — *In the Name of Satan*. Nashville, TN: Thomas Nelson, 1996.

Bob Larson — *Larson's Book of Spiritual Warfare*. Nashville, TN: Thomas Nelson, 1999.

Anton Szandor LaVey — *Satan Speaks!* Venice, CA: Feral House, 1998.

Anton Szandor LaVey — *The Satanic Bible*. New York: Avon, 1977.

Walter Martin — *The Kingdom of the Cults*. Rev., updated, and expanded ed. Minneapolis, MN: Bethany House, 1997.

Gareth J. Medway — *Lure of the Sinister: The Unnatural History of Satanism*. New York: New York University Press, 2001.

Michael Moynihan and Didrik Søderlind — *Lords of Chaos: The Bloody Rise of the Satanic Metal Underground*. Venice, CA: Feral House, 1998.

Debbie Nathan and Michael Snedeker — *Satan's Silence: Ritual Abuse and the Making of a Modern Witch Hunt*. New York: BasicBooks, 1995.

Allen Ottens and Rick Myer — *Satanism: Rumor, Reality, and Controversy*. Rev. ed. New York: Rosen, 1998.

Elaine Pagels — *The Origin of Satan*. New York: Random House, 1995.

George Palermo and Michele C. Del Re — *Satanism: Psychiatric and Legal Views.* Springfield, IL: Charles C. Thomas, 1999.

Bob Passantino and Gretchen Passantino — *Satanism.* Grand Rapids, MI: Zondervan, 1995.

Daniel Ryder — *Cover-Up of the Century: Satanic Ritual Crime and World Conspiracy.* Noblesville, IN: Ryder Publishing, 1996.

David K. Sakheim and Susan E. Devine — *Out of Darkness: The Controversy Over Satanism and Ritual Abuse.* San Francisco, CA: Jossey-Bass, 1997.

Jeffrey S. Victor — *Satanic Panic: The Creation of a Contemporary Legend.* Chicago: Open Court, 1993.

Periodicals

Bette L. Bottoms, Kathleen R. Diviak, and Suzanne L. Davis — "Jurors' Reactions to Satanic Ritual Abuse Allegations," *Child Abuse and Neglect,* September 1997.

Alexander Cockburn — "Katha's Silence," *Counterpunch,* October 26, 1999. Available at www.counterpunch.org/pollitt.html

Mary de Young — "Breeders for Satan: Toward a Sociology of Sexual Trauma Tales," *Journal of American Culture,* Summer 1996.

Mary de Young — "Speak of the Devil: Rhetoric in Claims-Making About the Satanic Ritual Abuse Problem," *Journal of Sociology and Social Welfare.* June 1996.

Shirley Emerson and Yvonne Syron — "Adolescent Satanism: Rebellion Masquerading as Religion," *Counseling and Values,* vol. 39, January 1995.

Gail Carr Feldman — "Satanic Ritual Abuse: A Chapter in the History of Human Cruelty," *Journal of Psychohistory,* Winter 1995.

Gary Alan Fine and Jeffrey S. Victor — "Satanic Tourism: Adolescent Dabblers and Identity Work," *Phi Delta Kappan,* September 1994.

S.C. Gwynne-Killeen — "I Saluted a Witch," *Time,* July 5, 1999.

Eagan Hunter — "Adolescent Attraction to Cults," *Adolescence,* vol. 33, September 22, 1998.

Marcia Ian — "The Unholy Family: From Satanism to the Chronos Complex," *Journal for the Psychoanalysis of Culture,* Fall 2000.

David P.H. Jones — "What Do Children Know About Religion and Satanism?" *Child Abuse and Neglect,* November 1997.

Garnet F. King and Beatrice Yorker — "Case Studies of Children Presenting with a History of Ritualistic Abuse," *Journal of Child and Adolescent Psychiatric Nursing,* April–June 1996.

Kenneth V. Lanning — "Investigator's Guide to Allegations of 'Ritual' Child Abuse," January 1992. Available at: www.religioustolerance.org/ra_rep03.htm

Katha Pollitt — "'Finality' or Justice?" *Nation,* October 18, 1999.

James Quan   "A Consolidation of SRA and False Memory Data,"
                          November 1996. Available at: www.iccom.com/
                          usrwwww/jlquan.connsldra.doc.

A.S. Ross   "Blame It on the Devil," *Redbook*, June 1994.

Kevin Sack   "Grim Details Emerge in Teen-Age Slaying Case," *New
                          York Times*, October 15, 1997.

Jeffrey S. Victor   "Satanic Cults' Ritual Abuse of Children: Horror or
                          Hoax?" *USA Today*, November 1993.

Richard Webster   "Speak of the Devil: Tales of Satanic Abuse in Contem-
                          porary England," *New Statesman*, February 27, 1998.

Timothy J. Zeddies   "Adolescent Satanism: An Intersubjective and Cultural
                          Perspective," *Journal for the Psychoanalysis of Culture*, Fall
                          2000.

Index